animal hatchdoodles

modern minimalist color-in art pages

get amazing results with just one color
or go wild with a full palette

discover the power of cross hatching
with pages formatted to trim into 8"x10" frames
color in, stand back and watch your art take form

de-stress and enjoy your color journey with
hatchdoodles

dedication
i dedicate this book to my amazing children and wife.
their loving support and sometimes brutal
critique all helped shape our new hatchdoodle format
and this book into its current form.

ISBN-13: 978-1547188802
ISBN-10: 1547188804

hatchdoodle
tips n tricks

* do one just with black to get used to this way of coloring in

* place a sheet of paper behind page to stop any color bleeding

* color upward /// lines first. these generally are lighter in color

* color your downward \\\ lines last which generally are darker

* follow a line from start to end even if it crosses another
    this helps build up color in all the right spots

* smaller dots will be in line with either a \ or / and can be colored accordingly

* placing a ruler or edge of a sheet of paper under a line will help you see any
    other lines in the same row

* enjoy experimenting
    use alternating colors
    highlight each line cross with a metallic pen
    shade in between lines for a fuller effect
    patch hatch the paper before line coloring

* above all.
# have fun

animal list
arctic fox, basset, beagle, bear, bunny, butterfly, cat, cow, deer, dinosaur, dolphin
duck, eagle, elephant, flamingo, fox, frog, giraffe, gorilla, hippopotamus, horse
lamb, lion, owl, panda, parrot, penguin, pig, polar bear, raccoon, shark, tiger, zebra

ISBN-13: 978-1547188802
ISBN-10: 1547188804

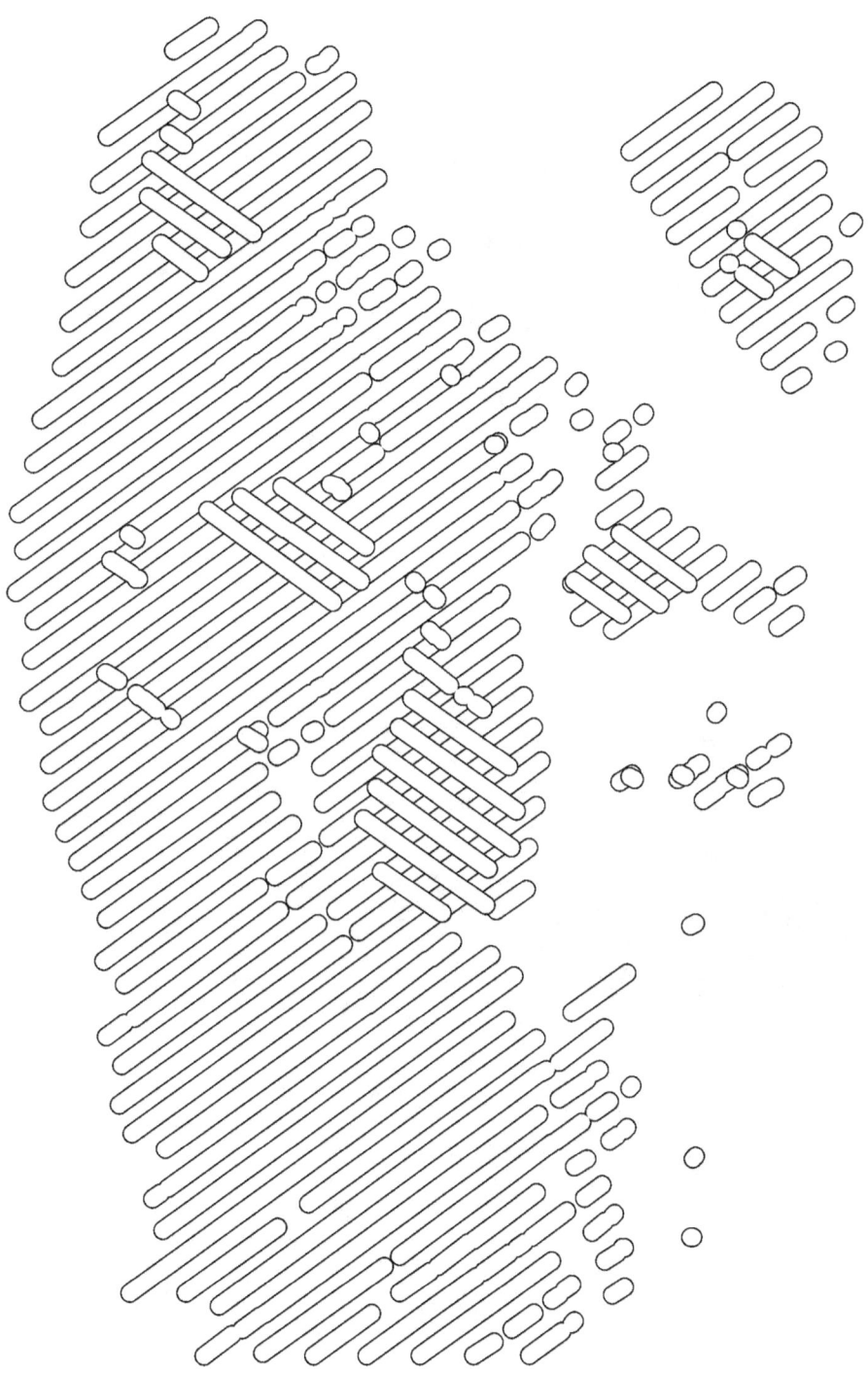

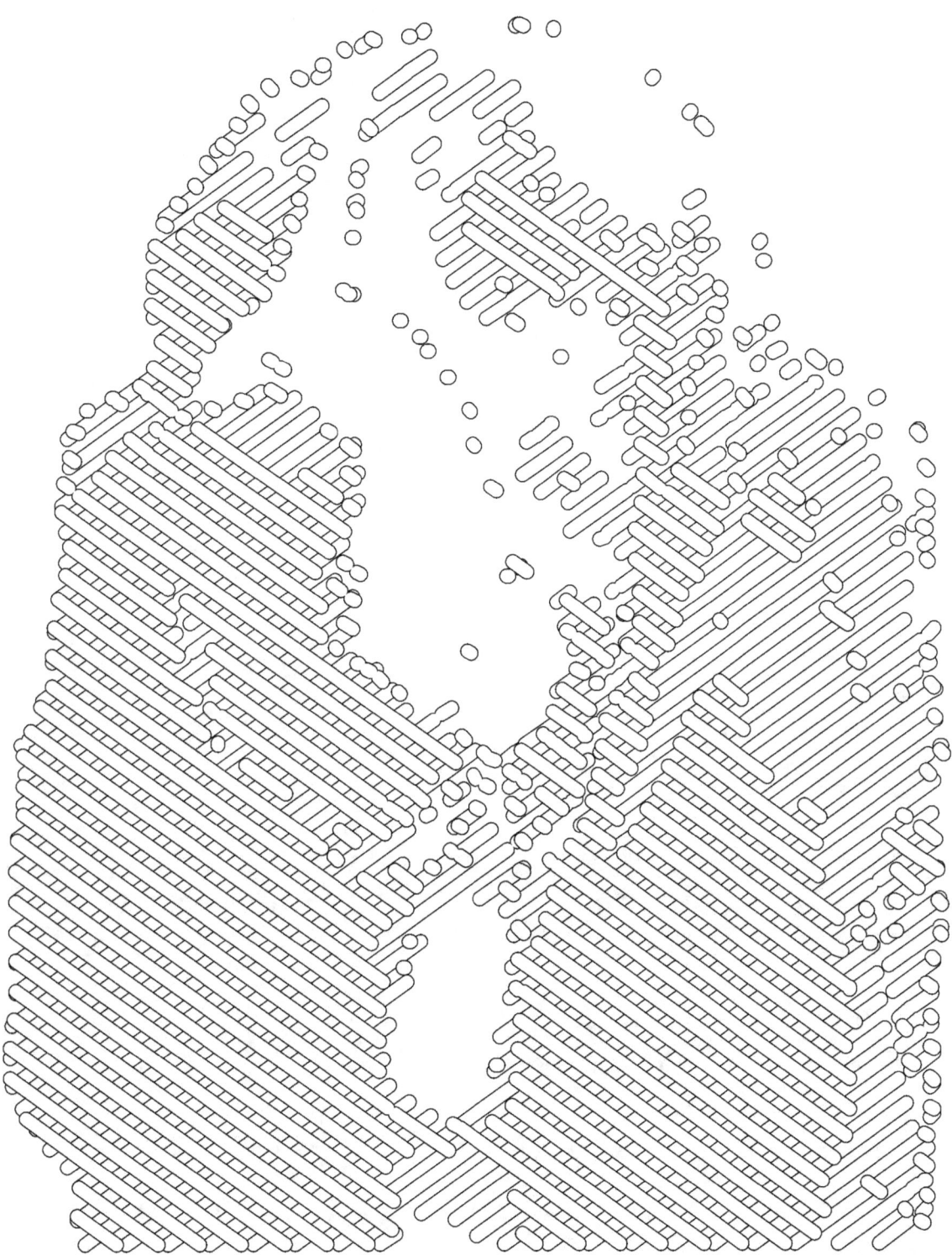

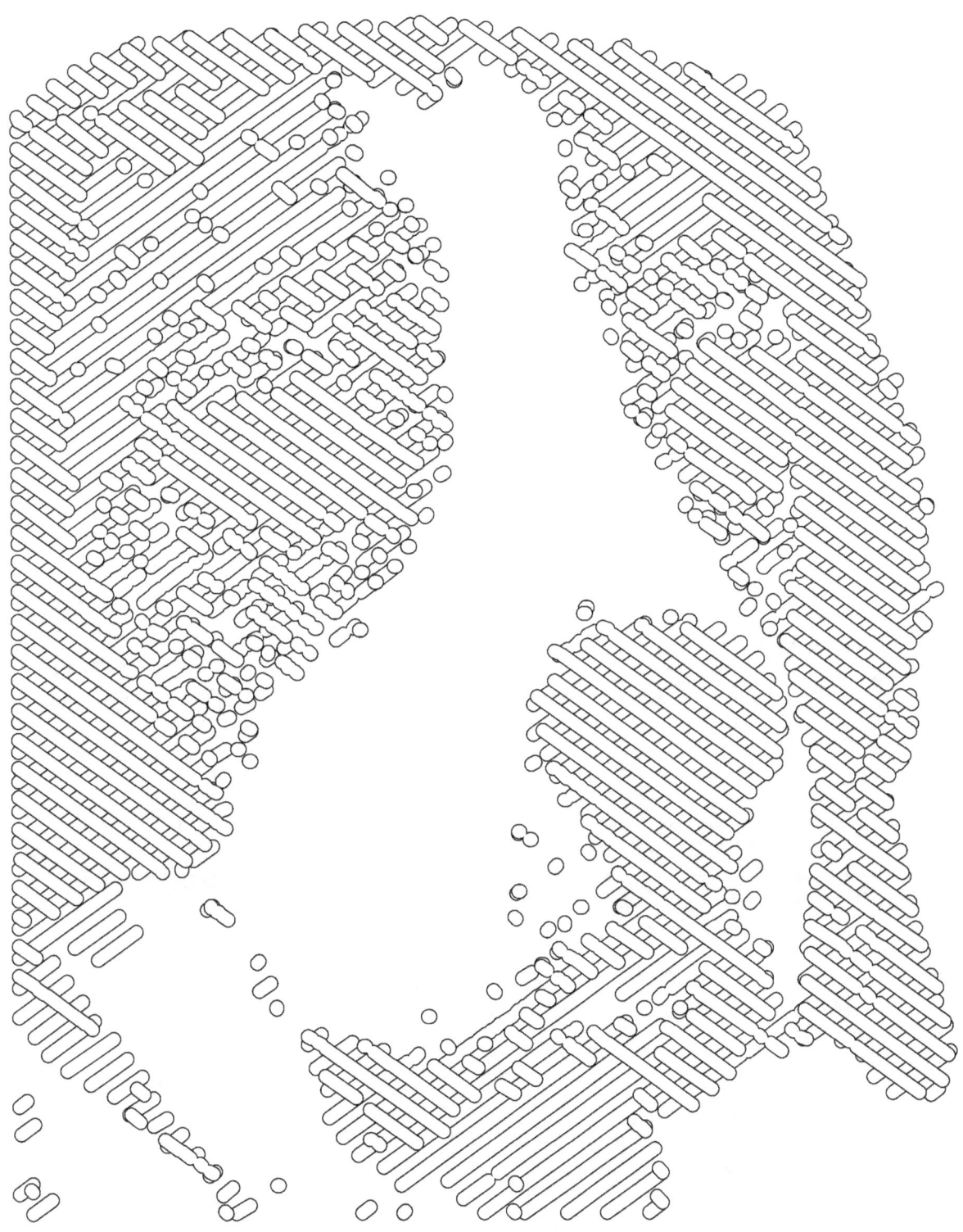

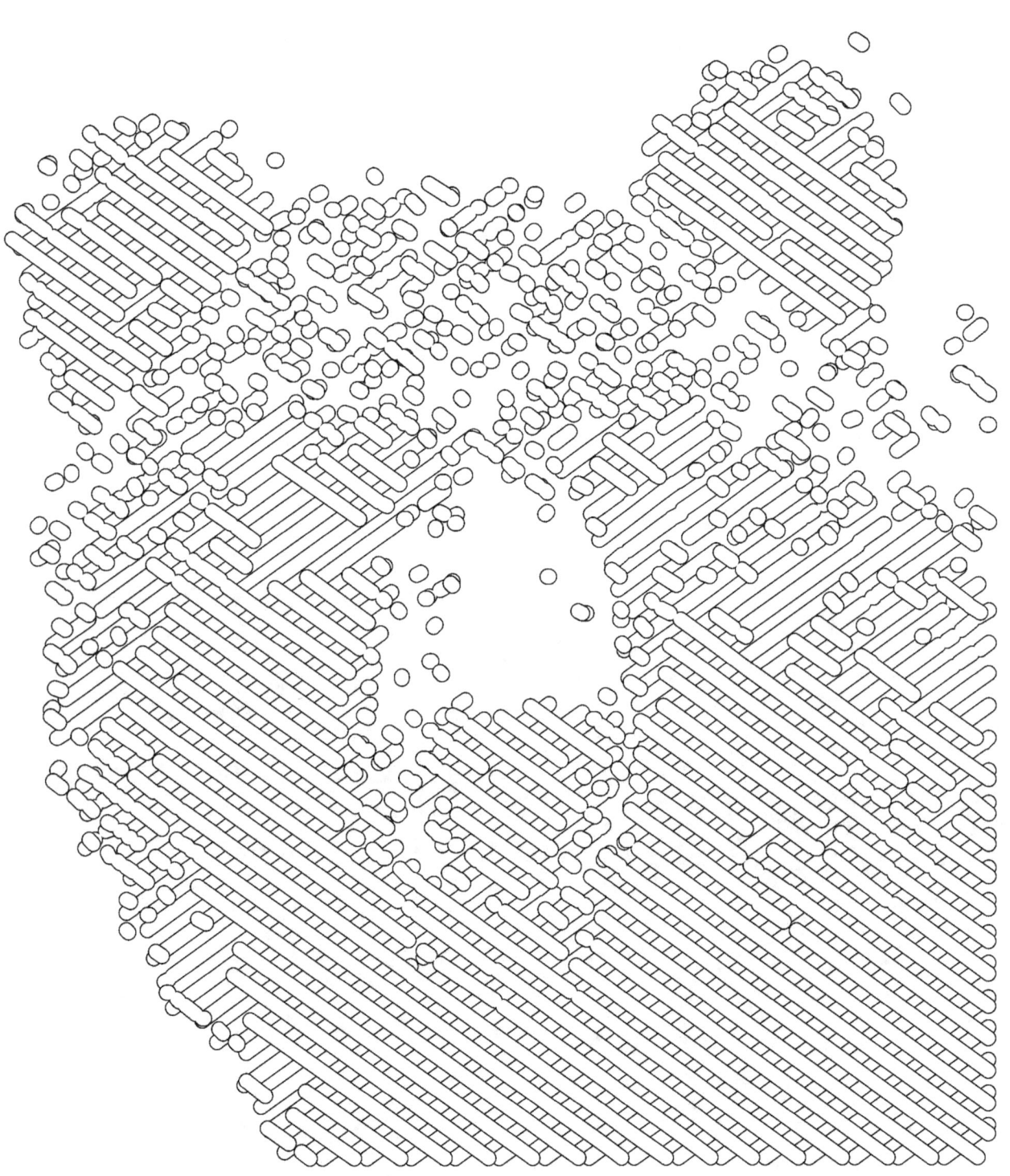

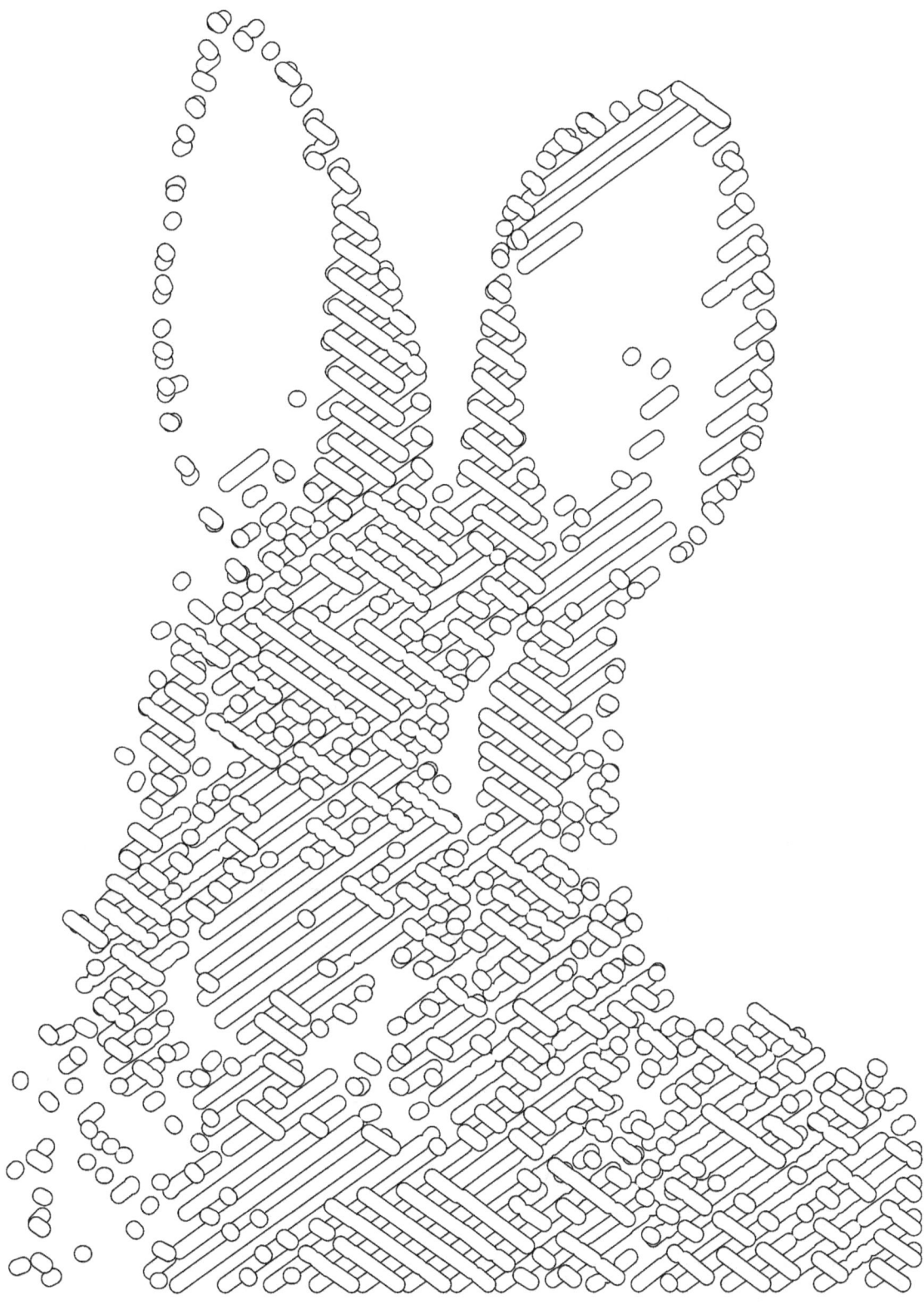

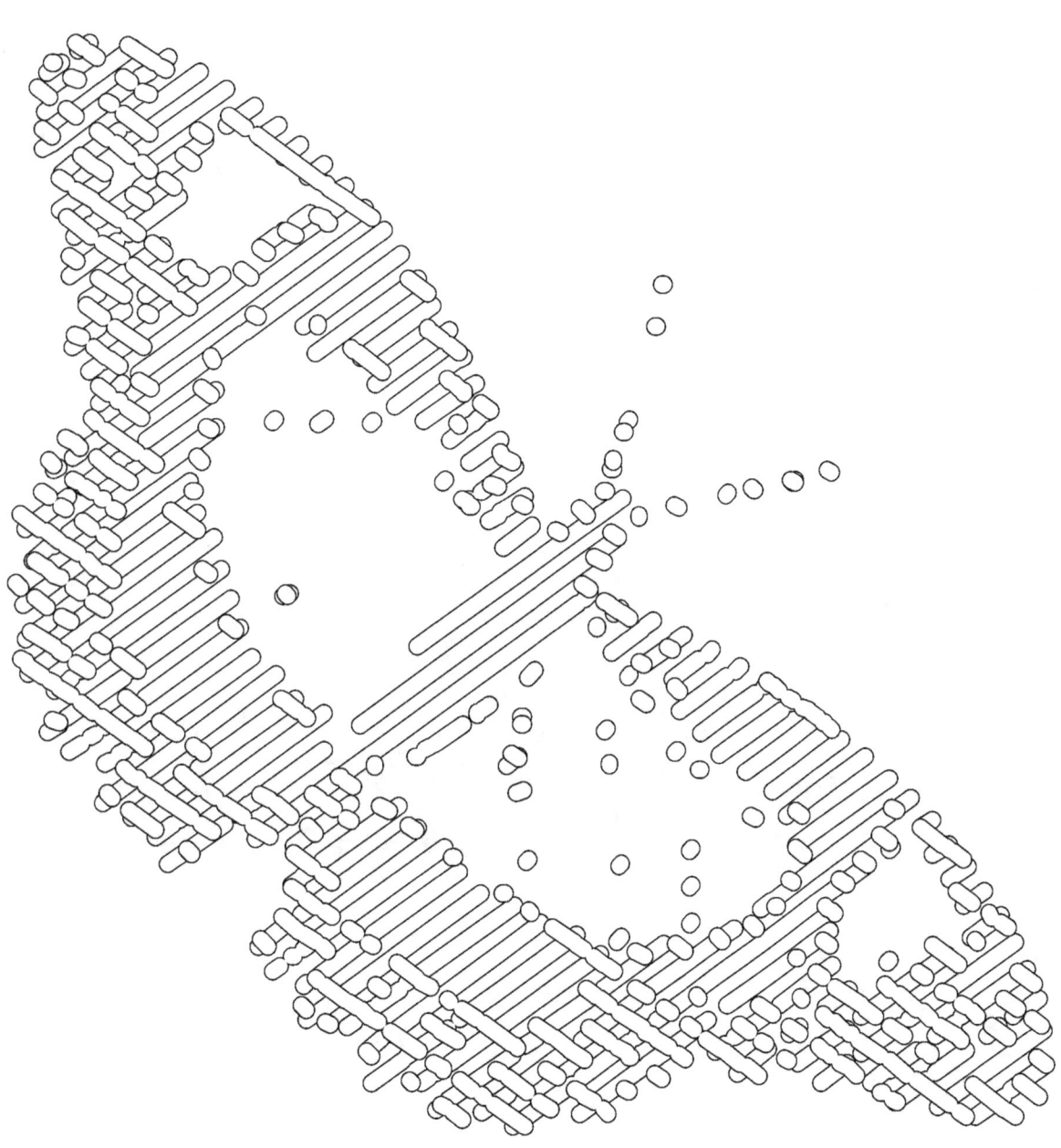

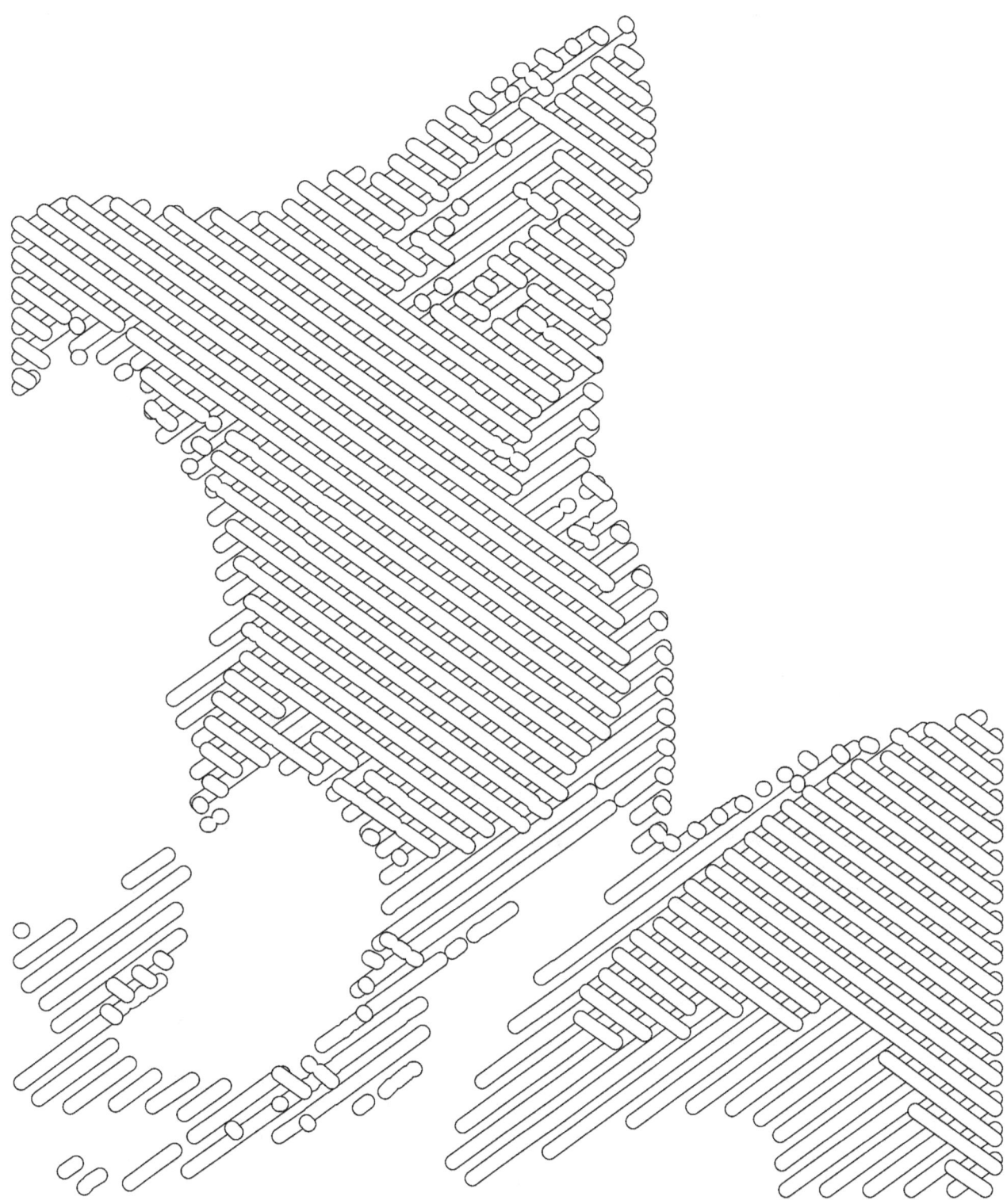

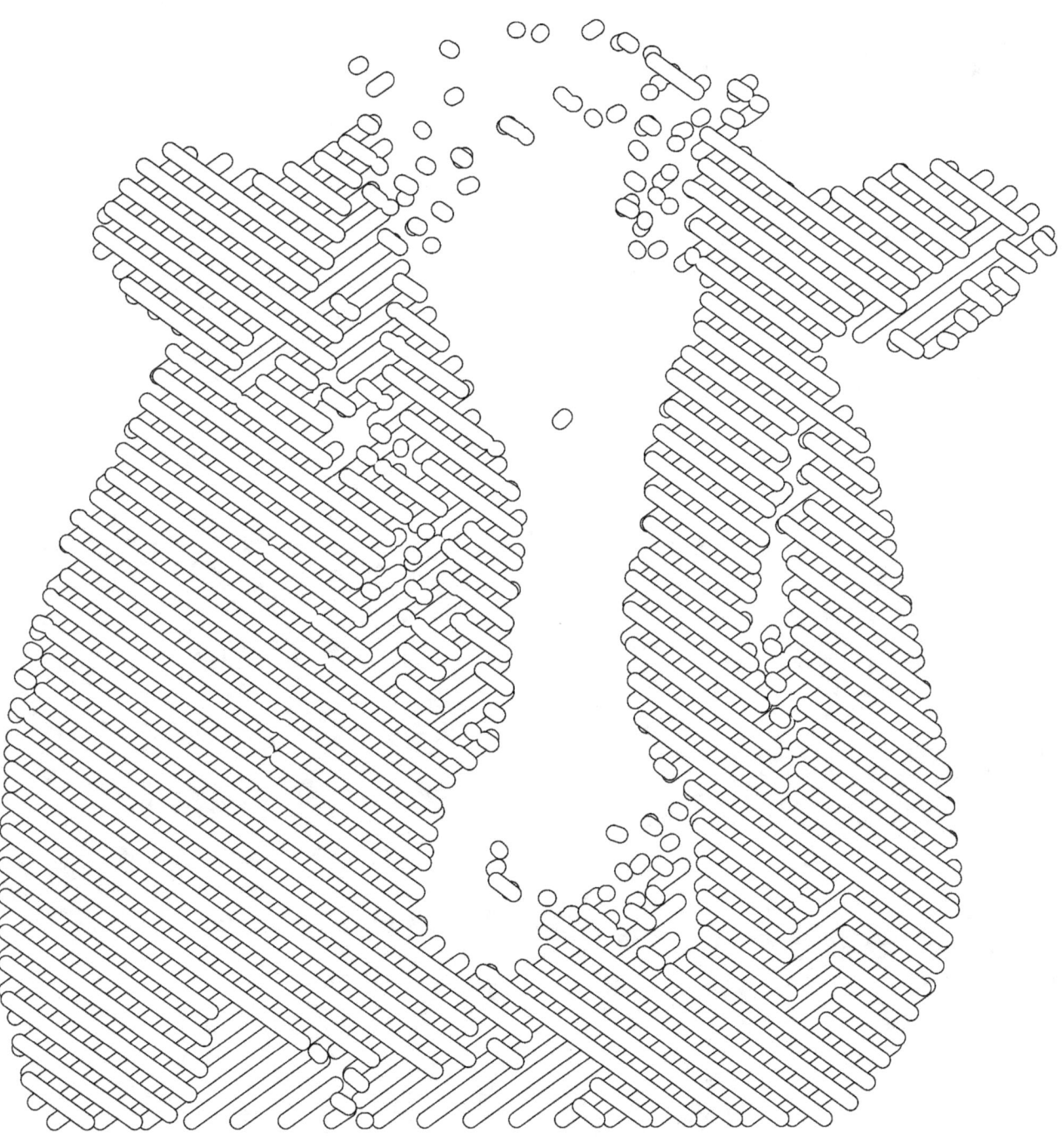

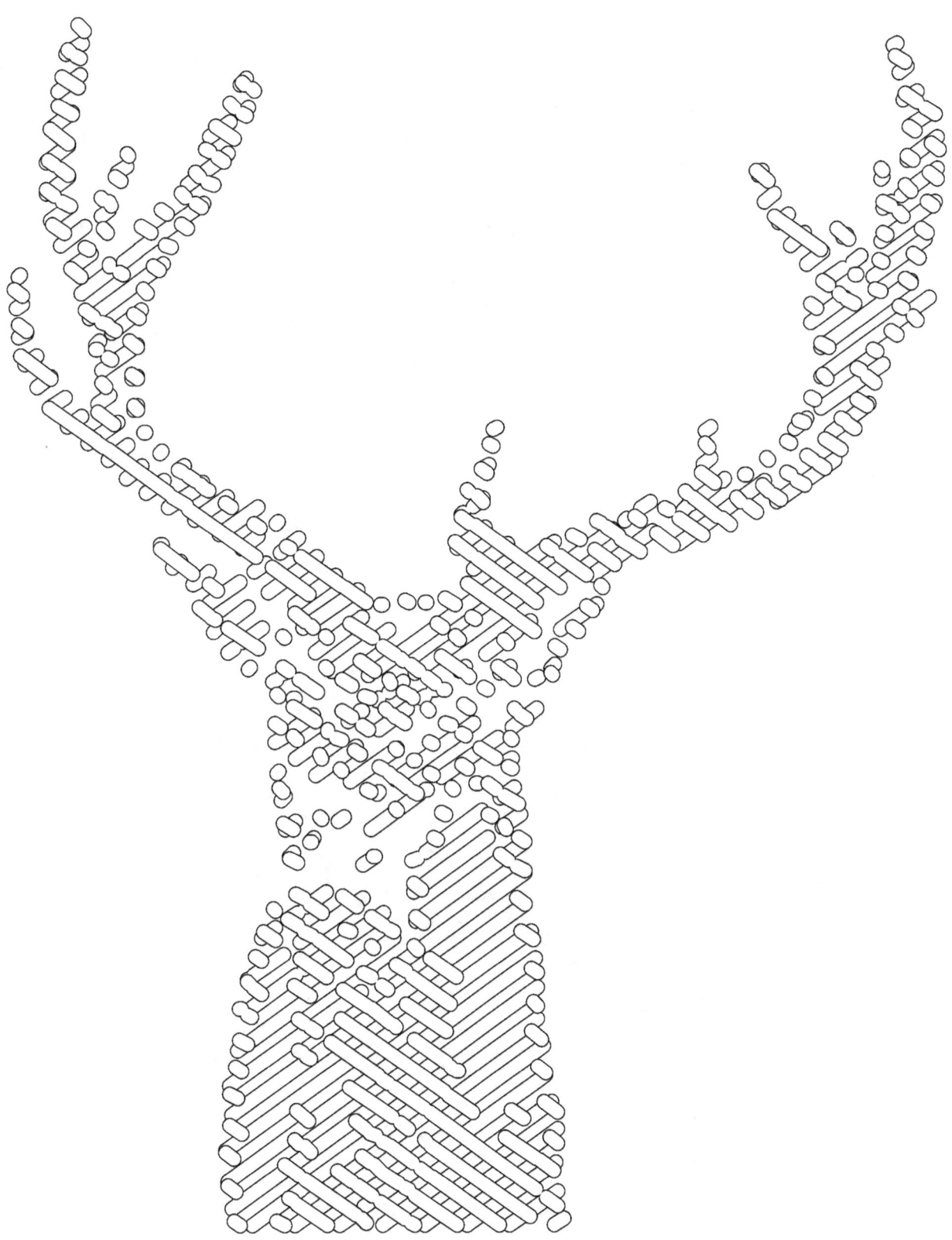

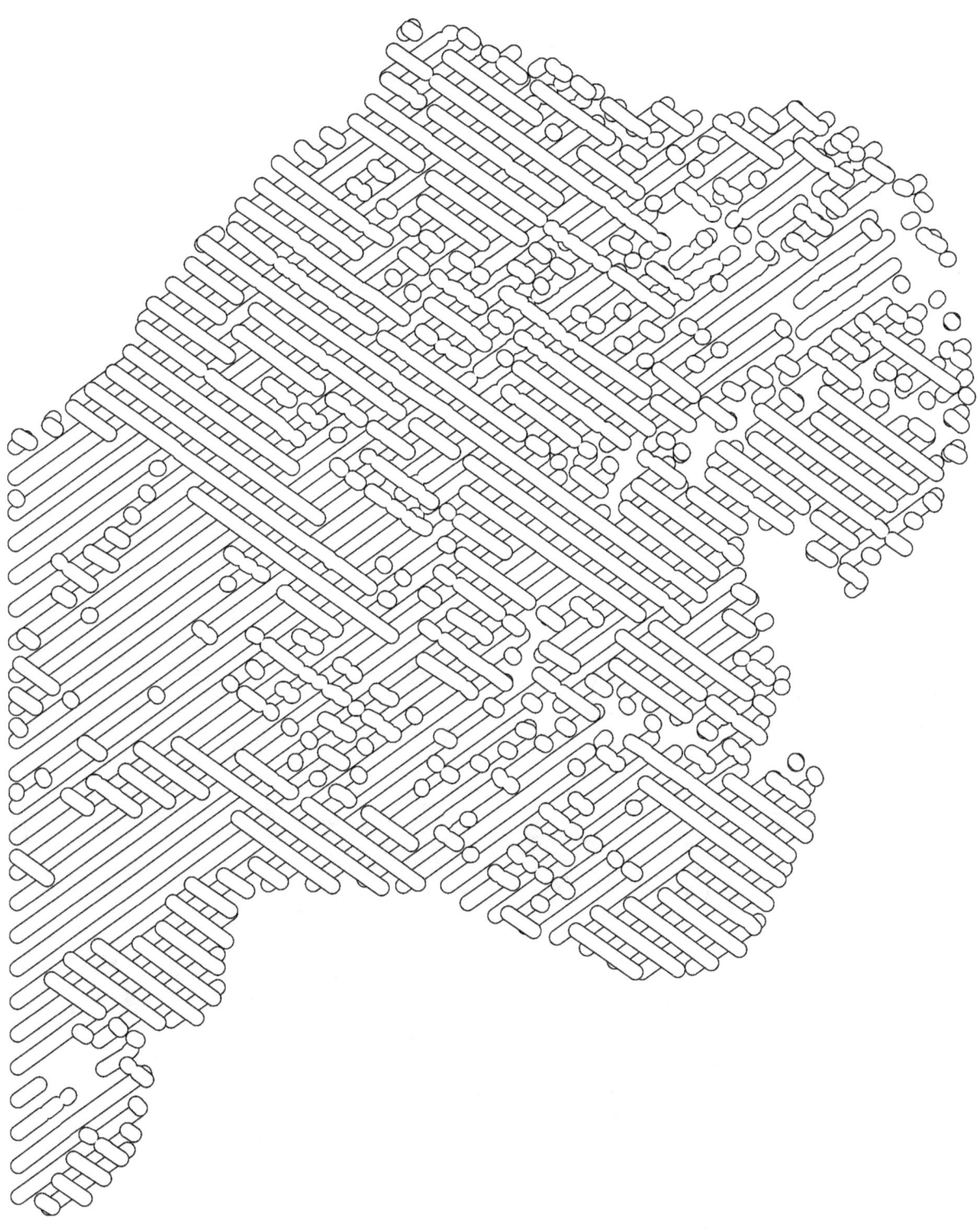

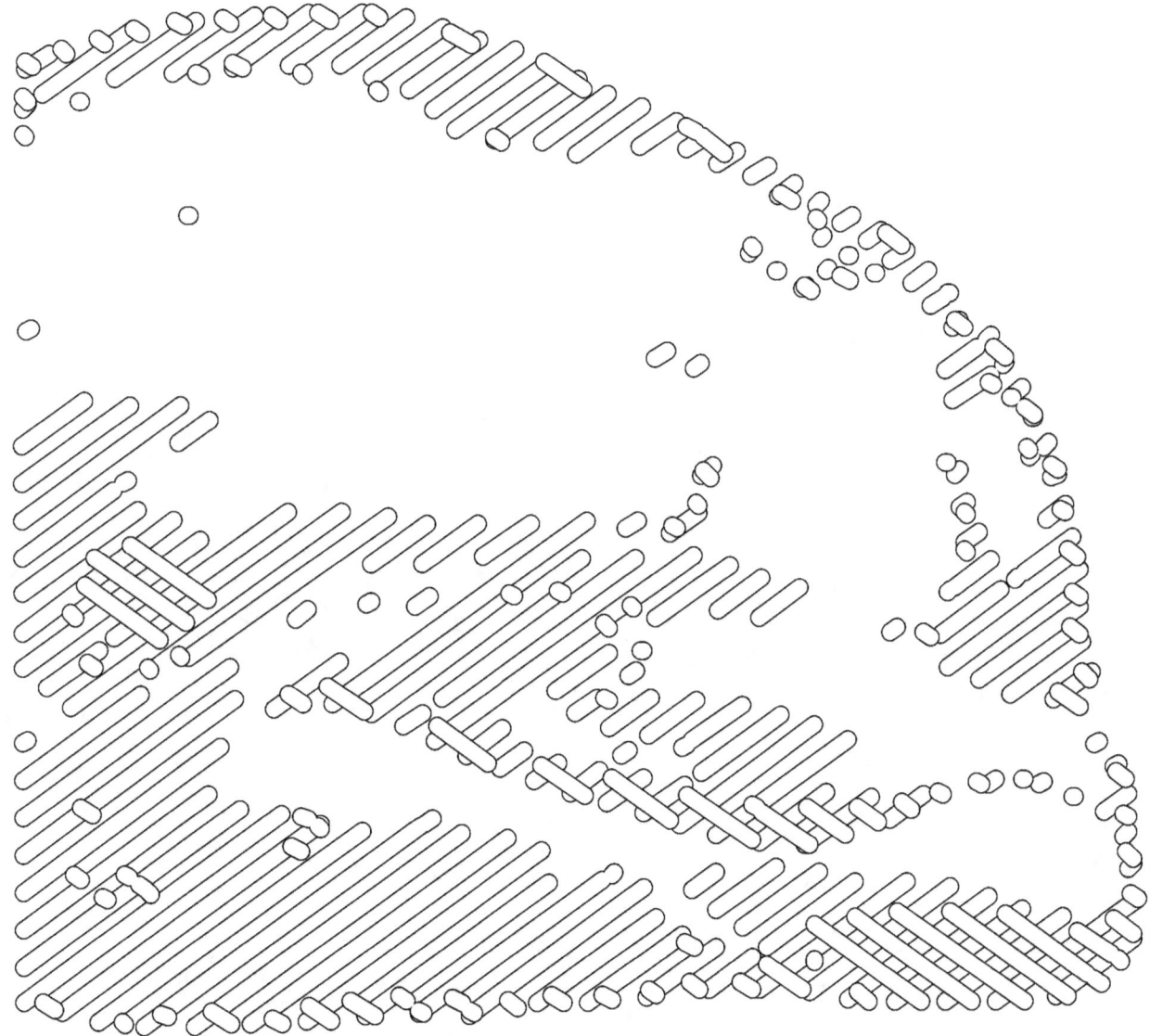

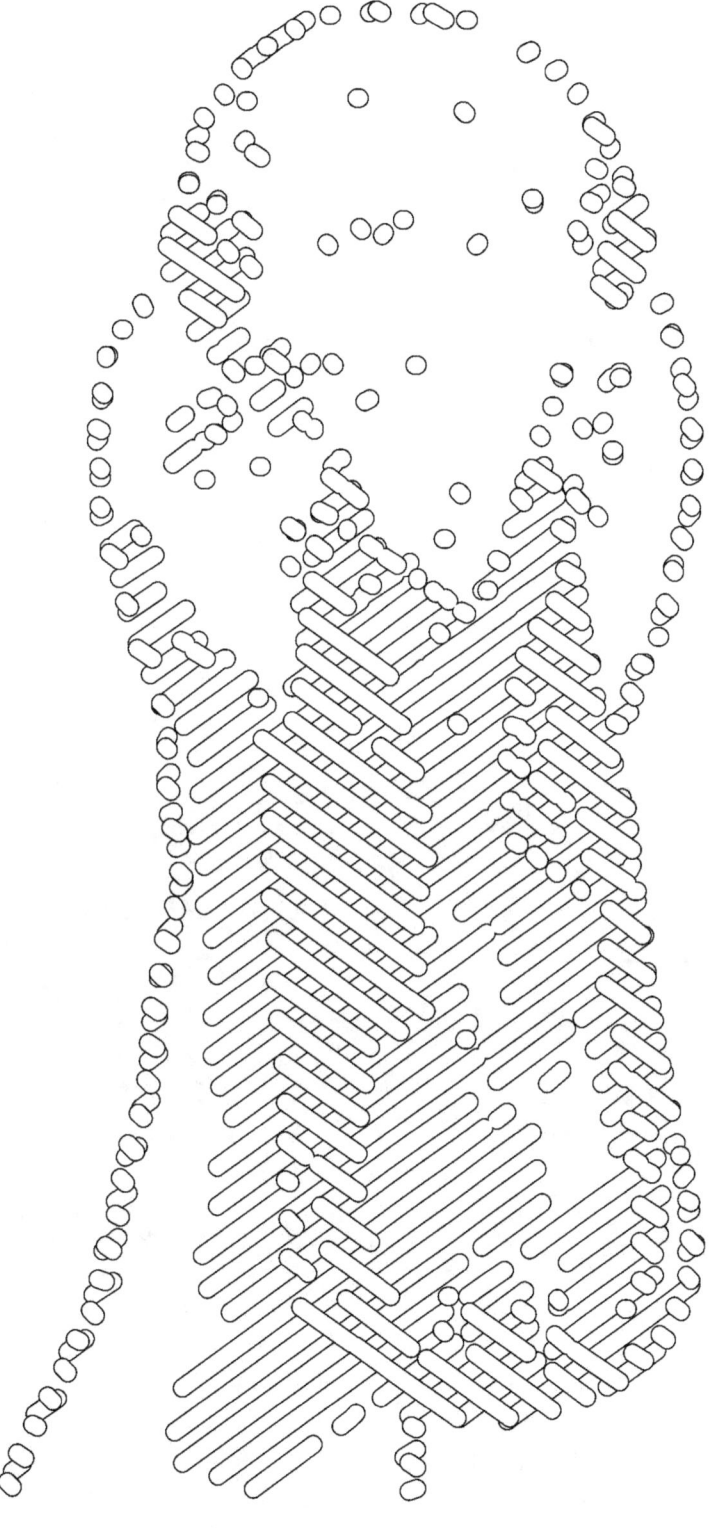

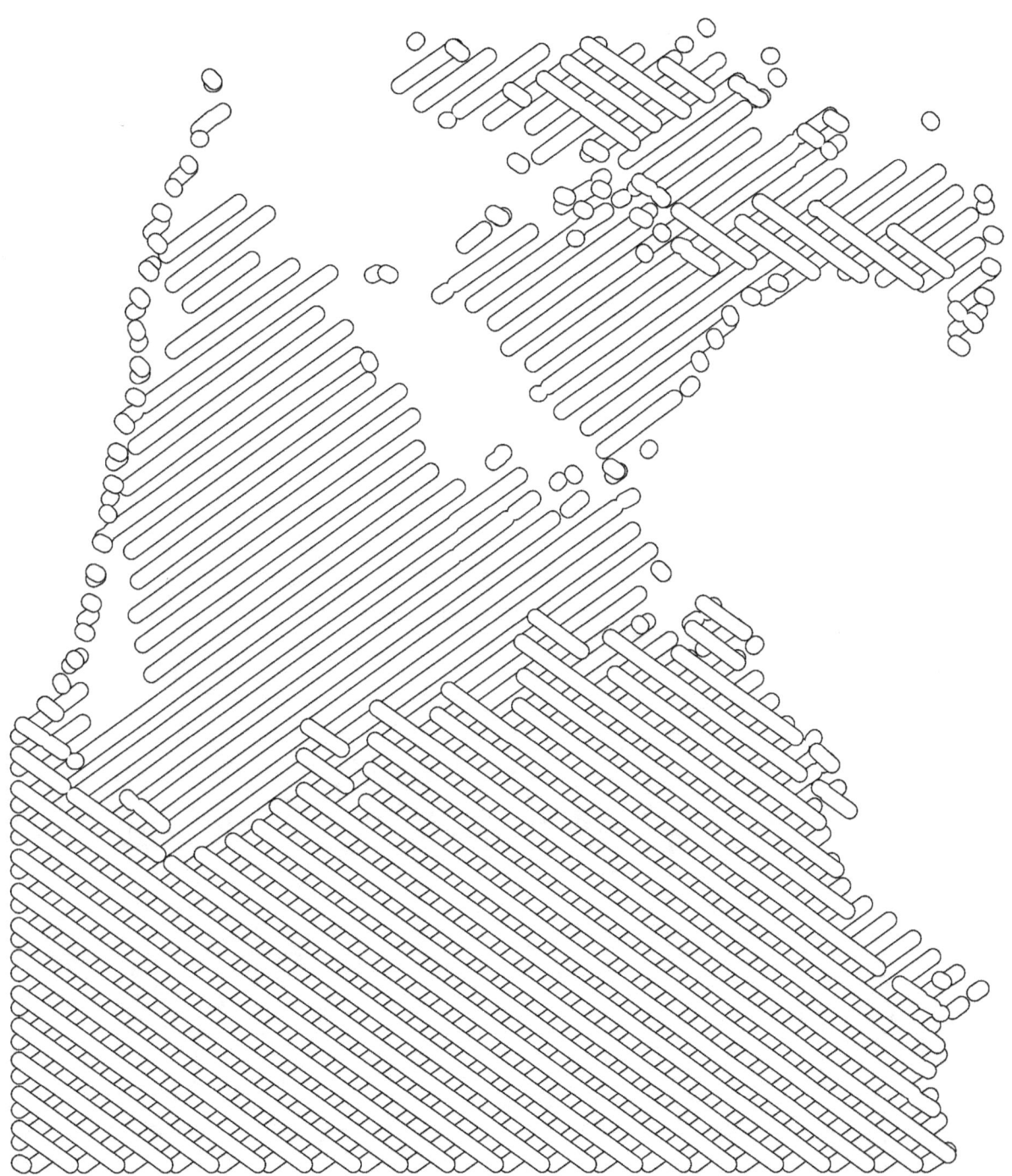

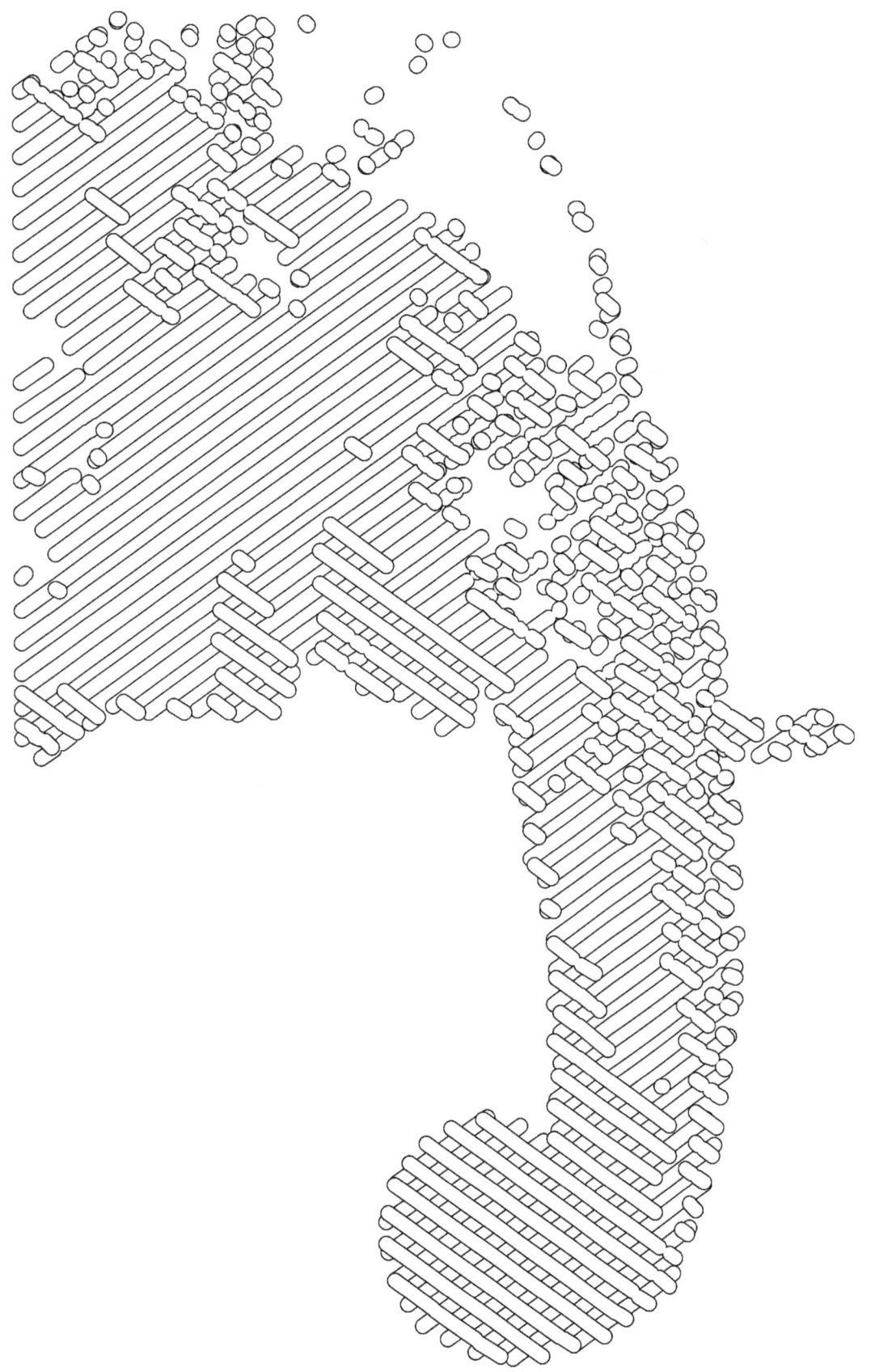

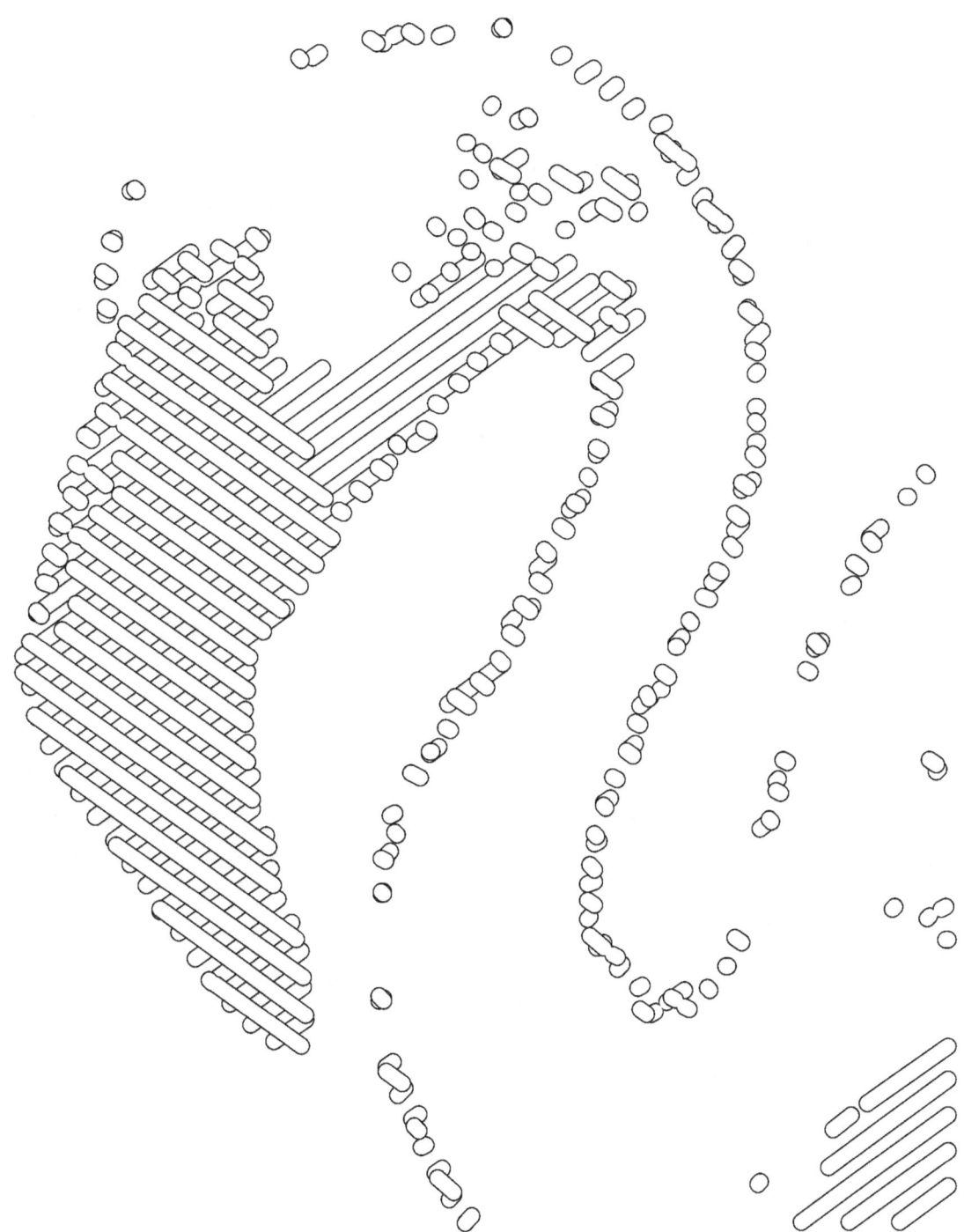

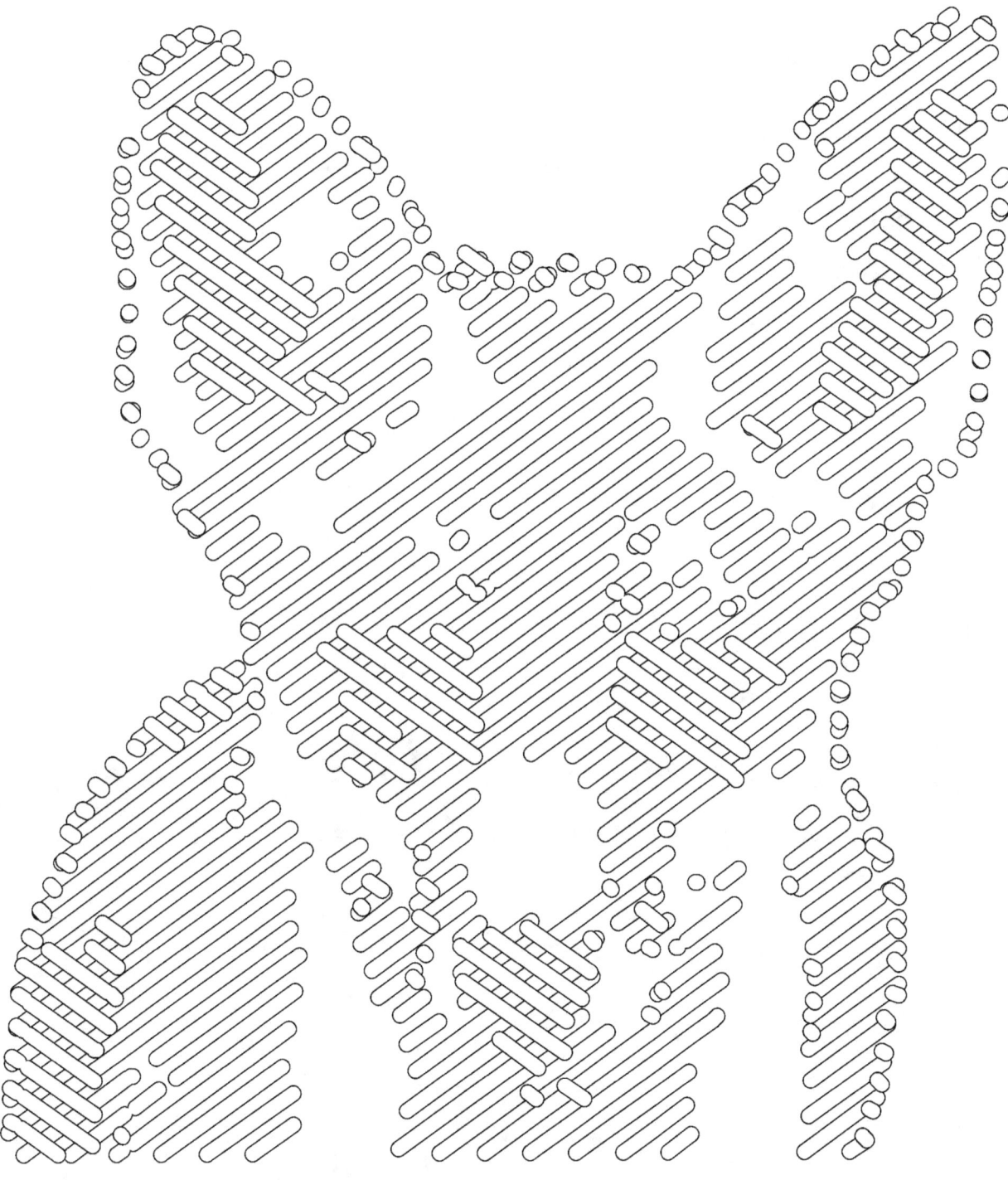

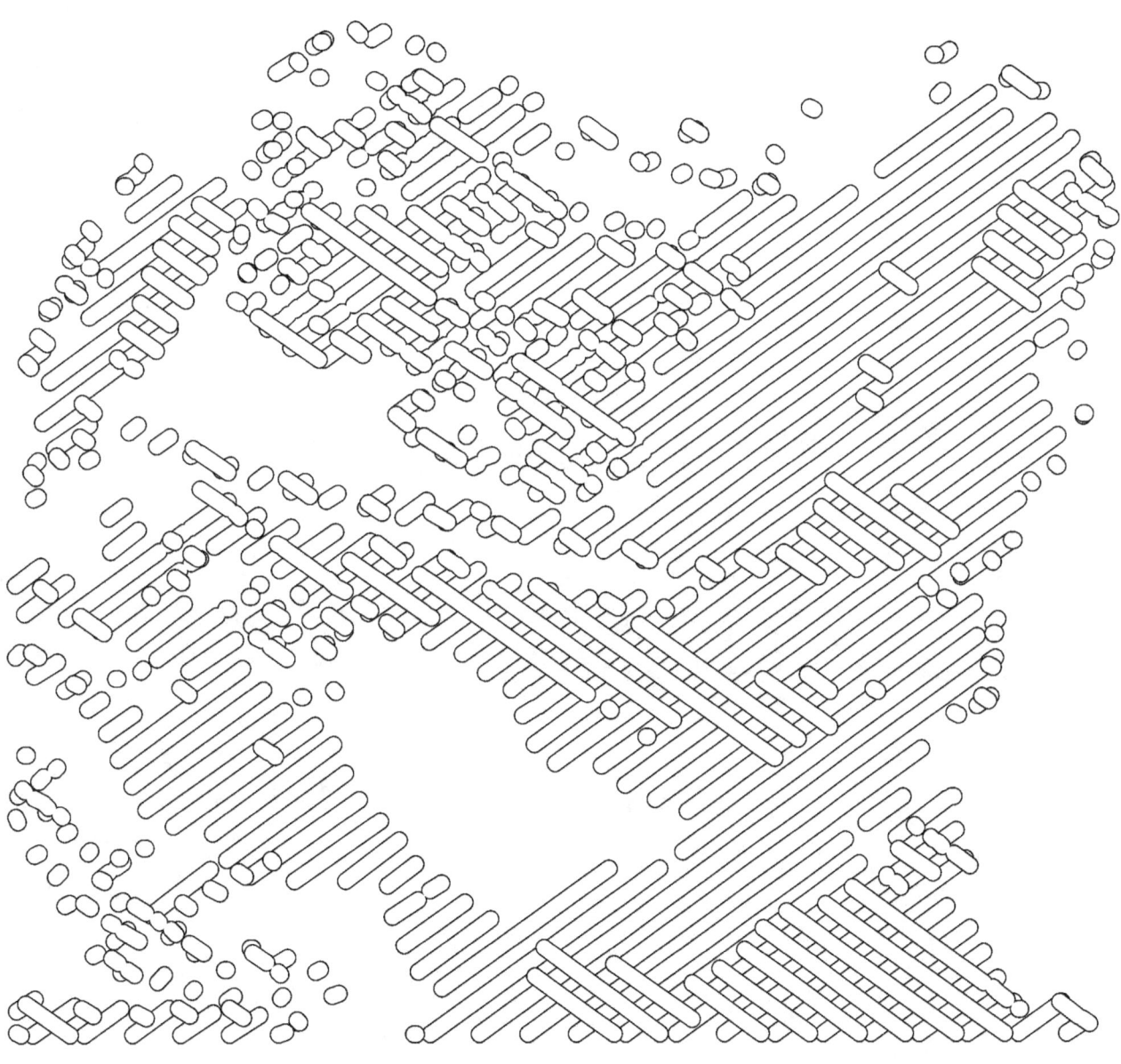

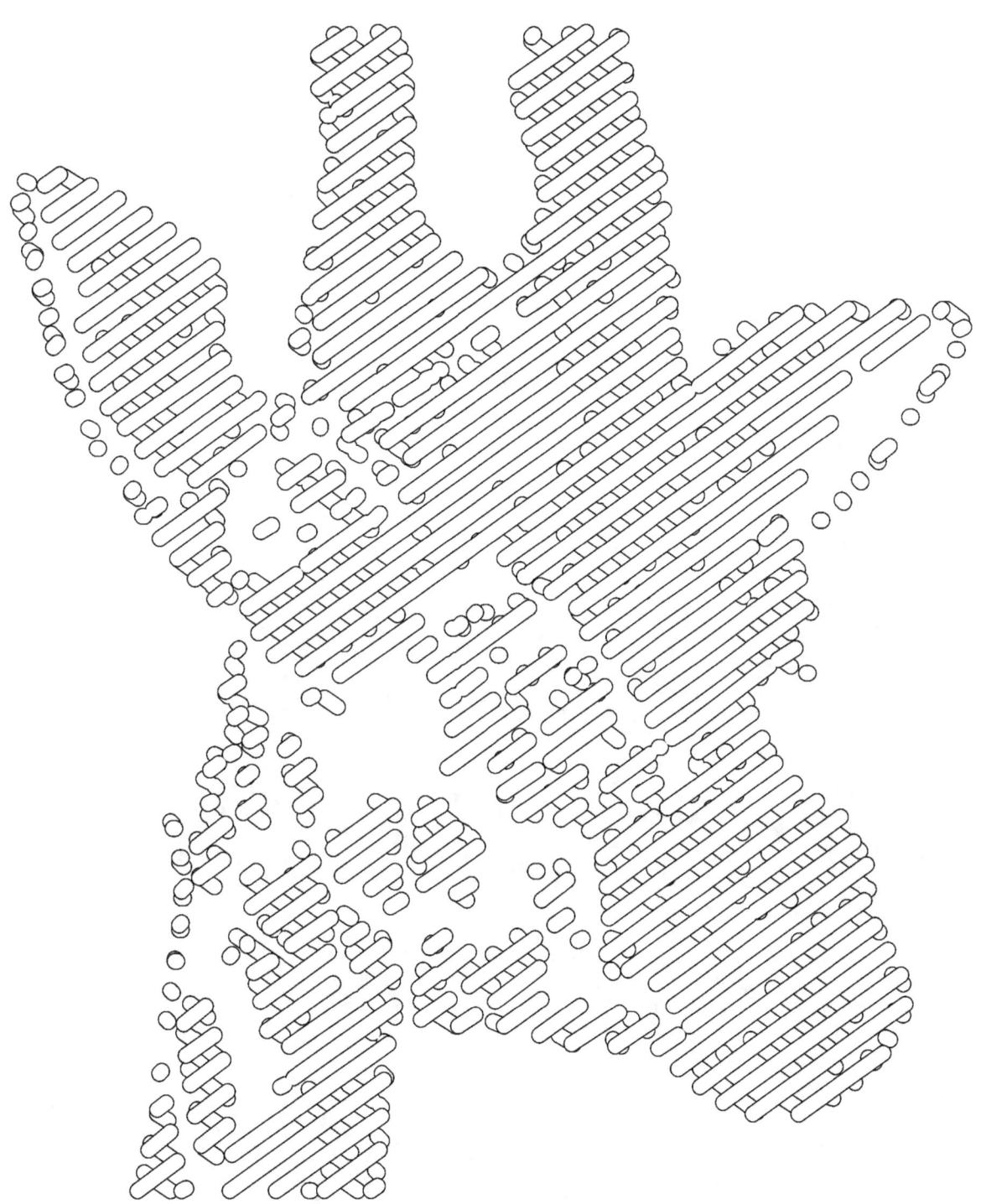

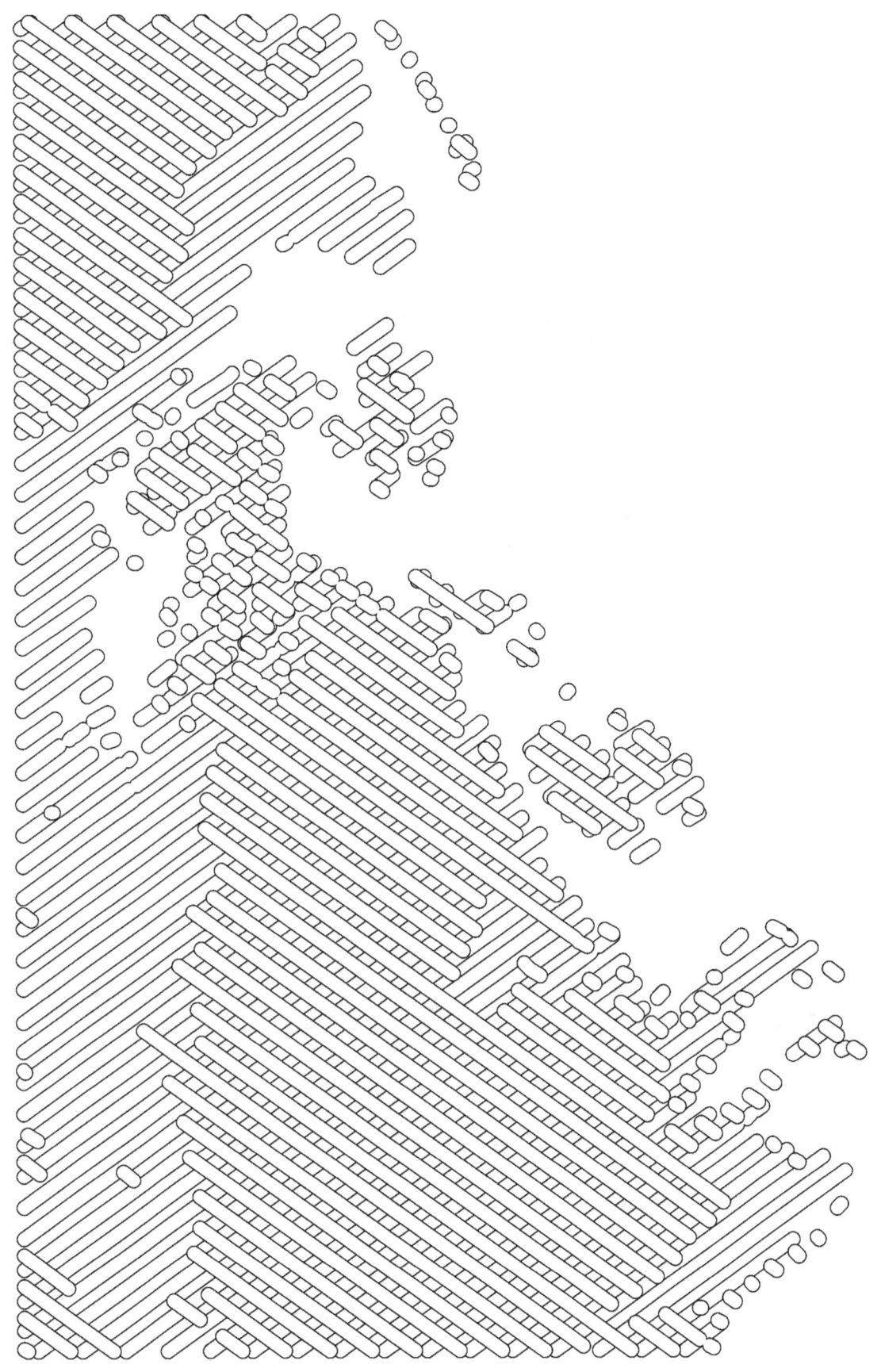

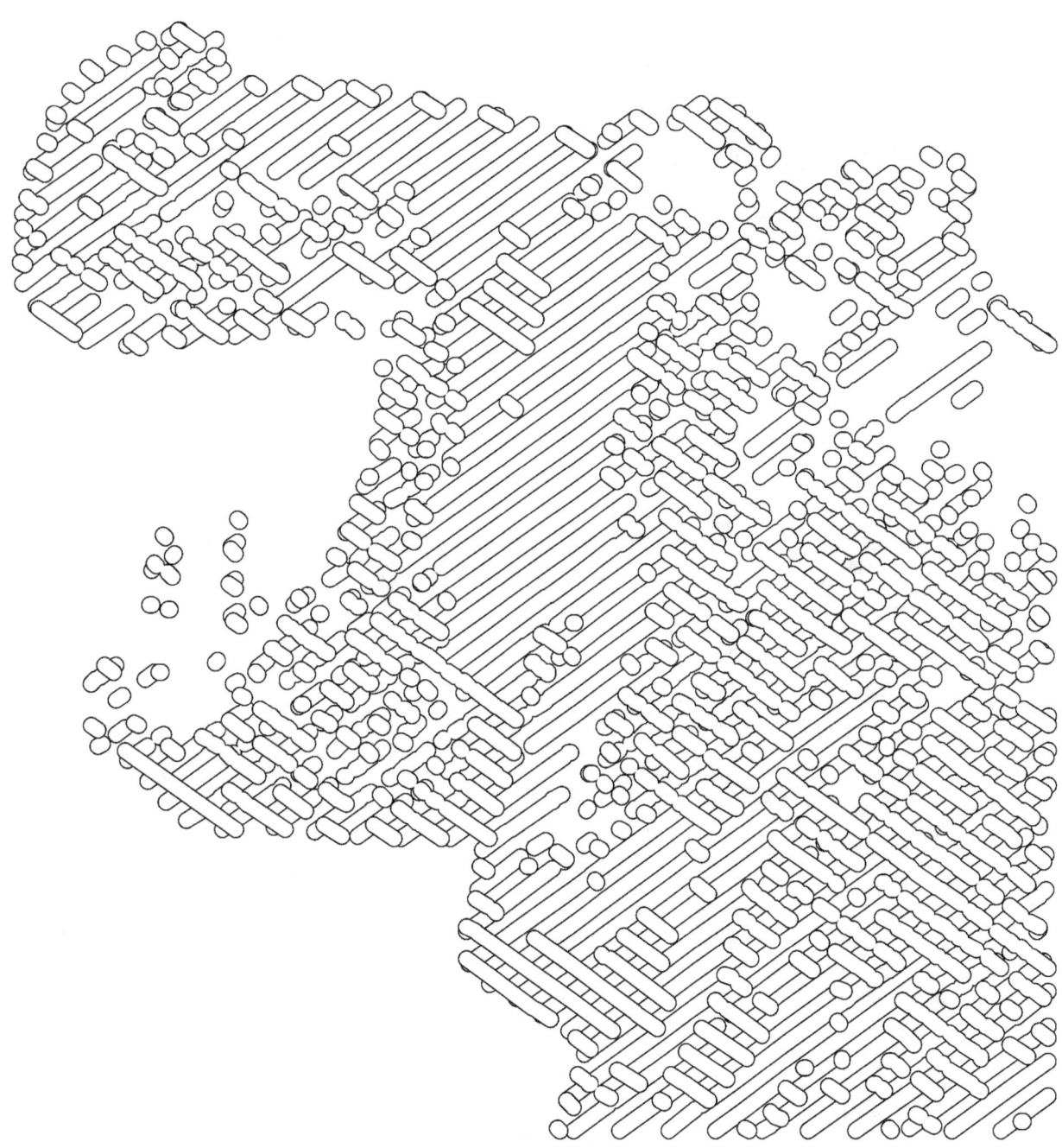

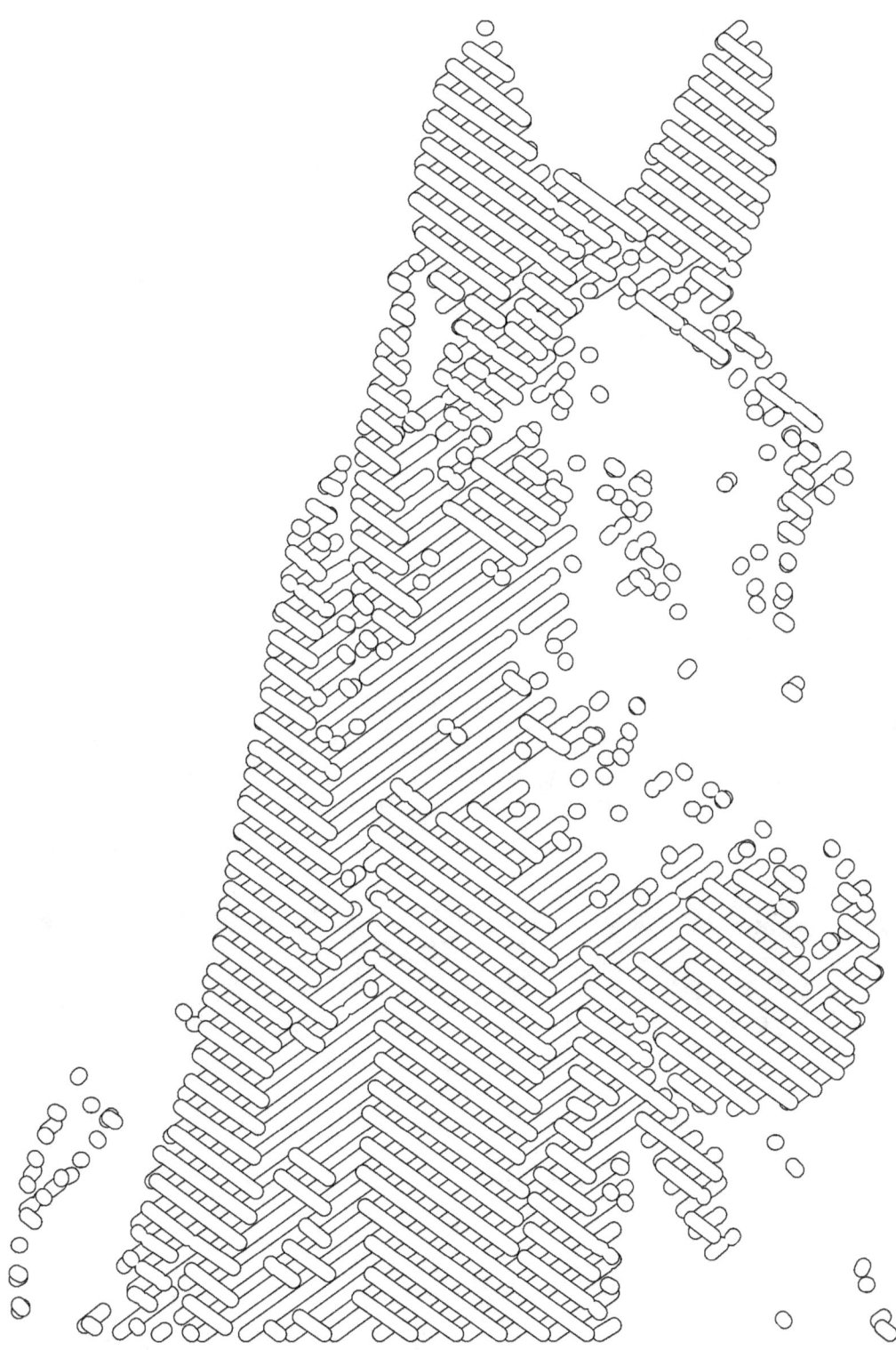

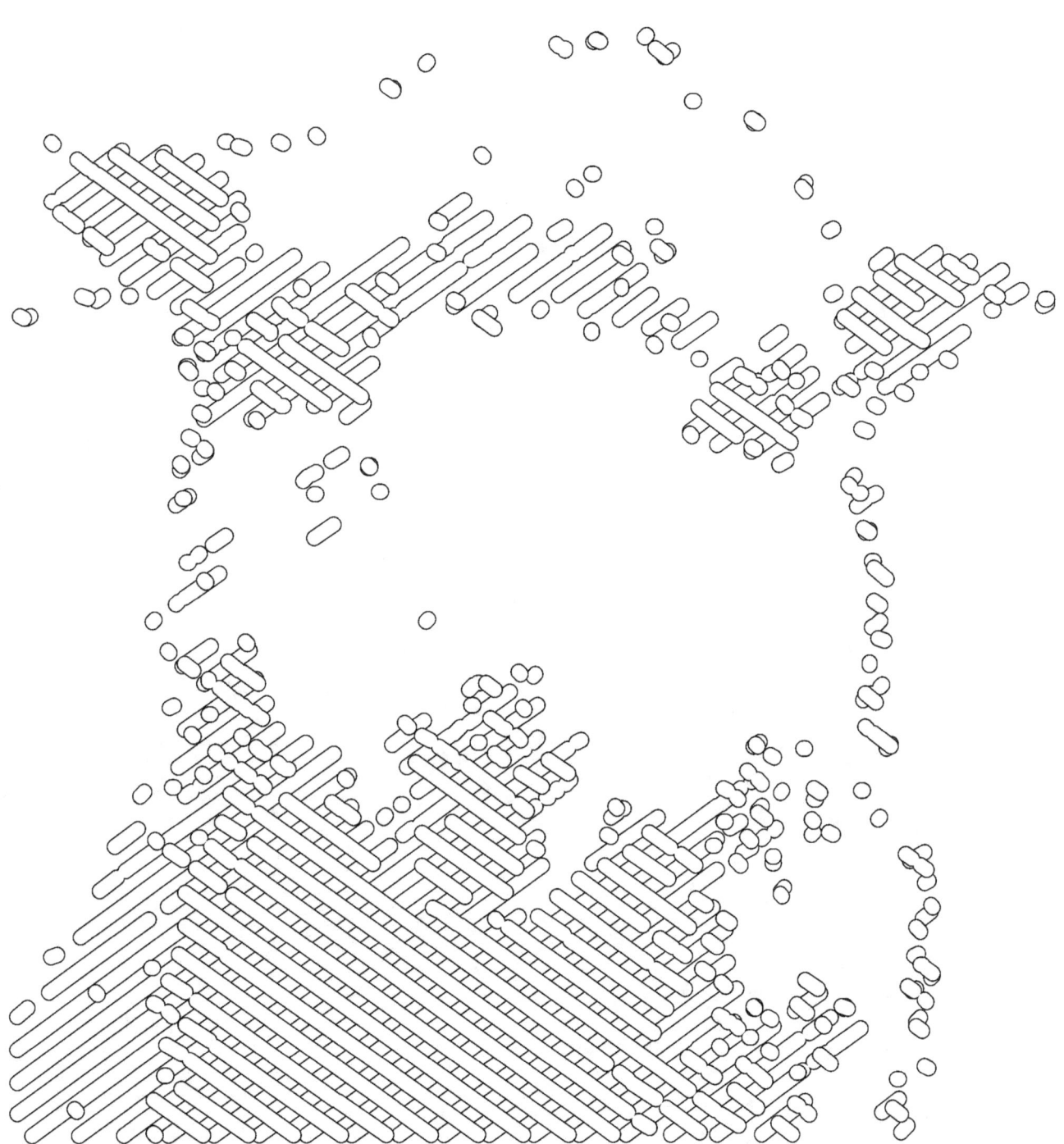

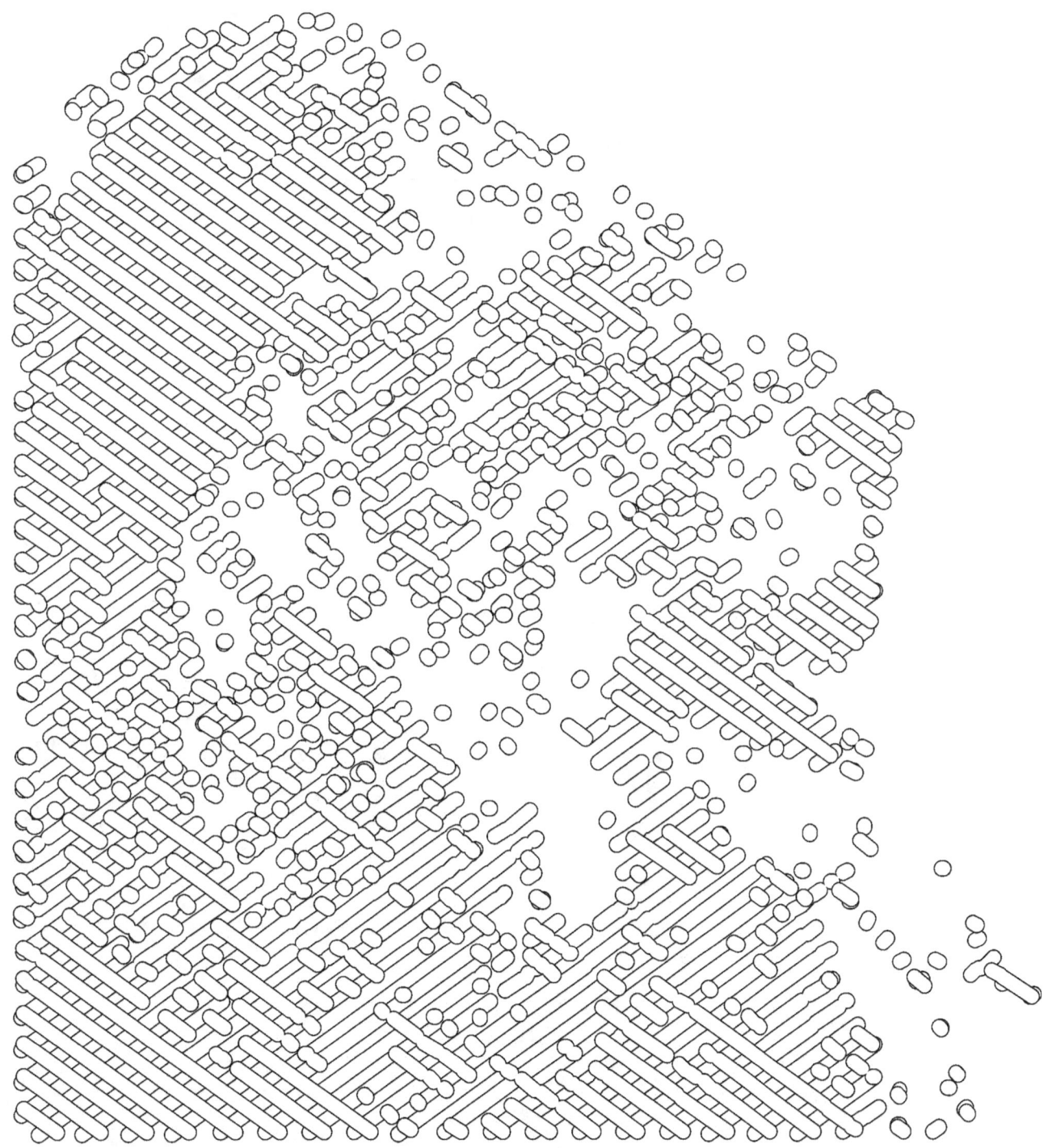

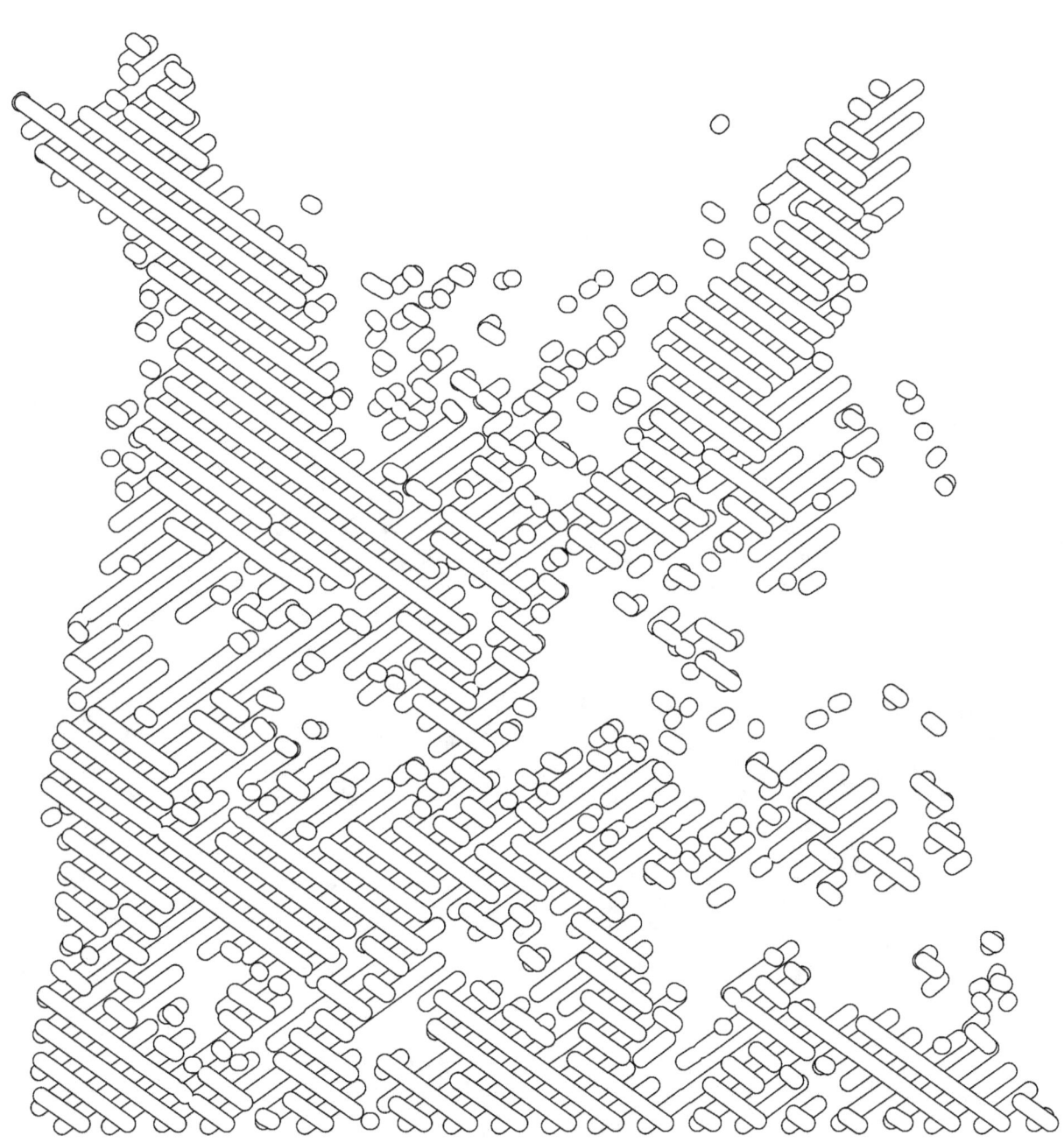

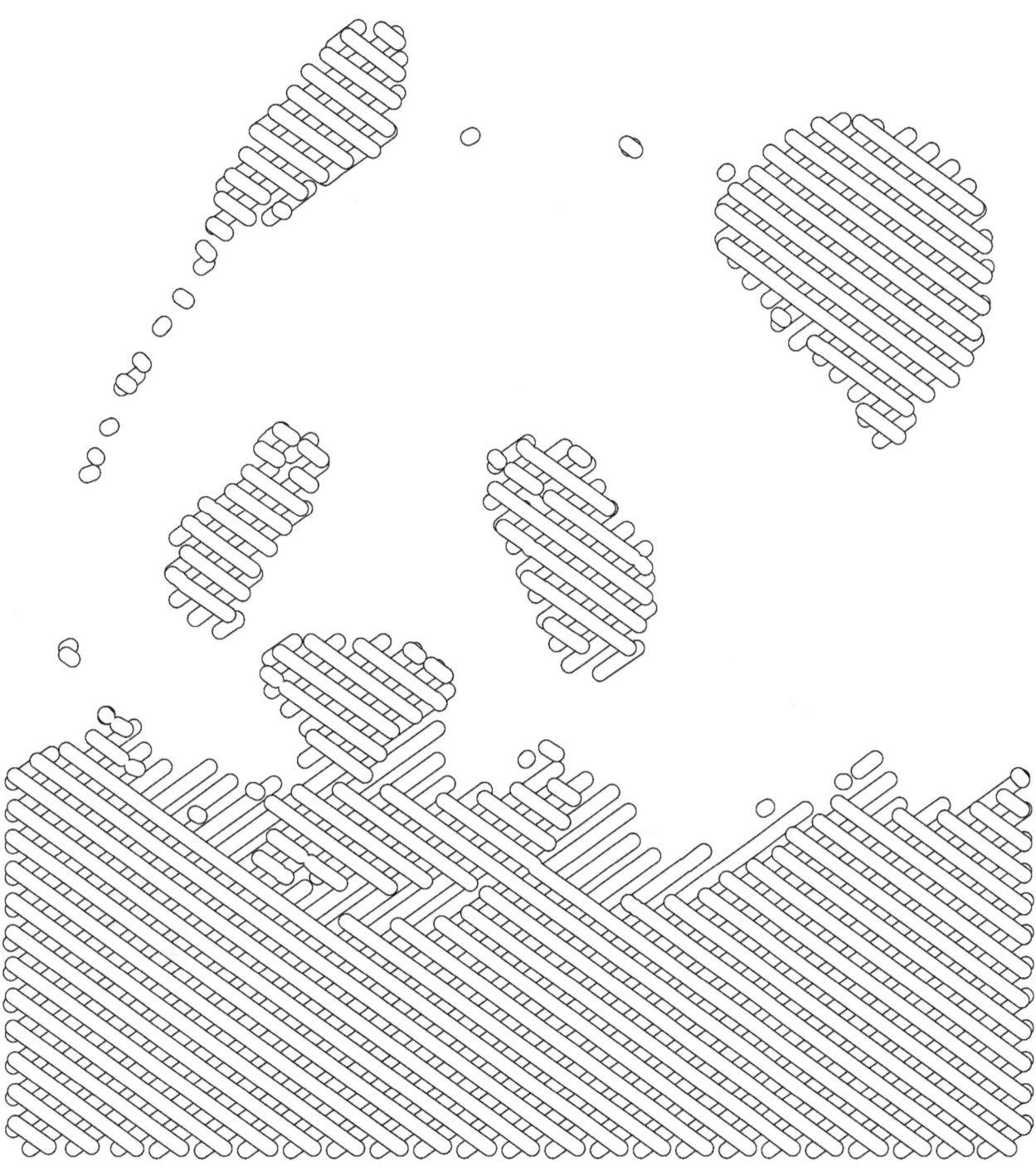

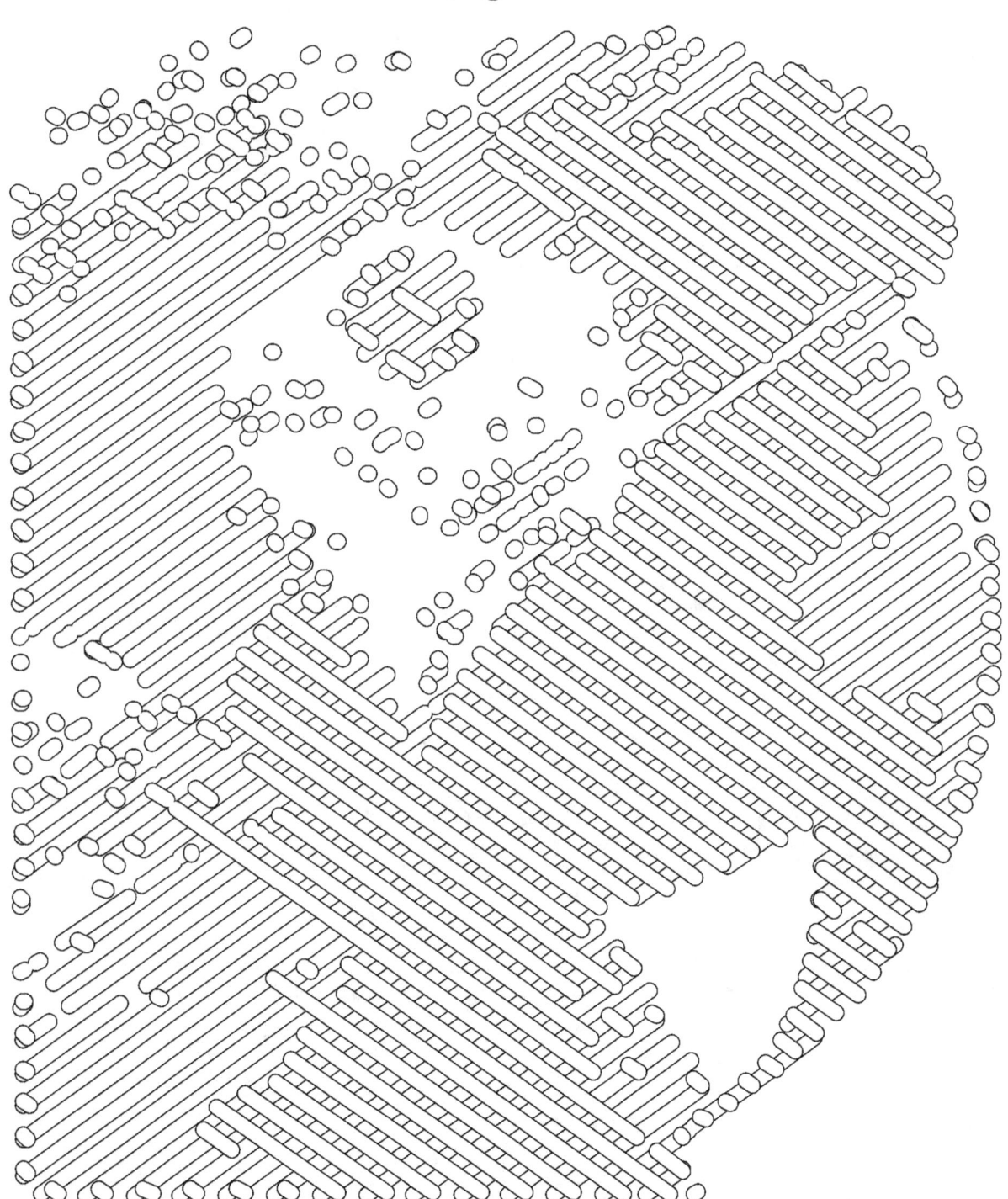

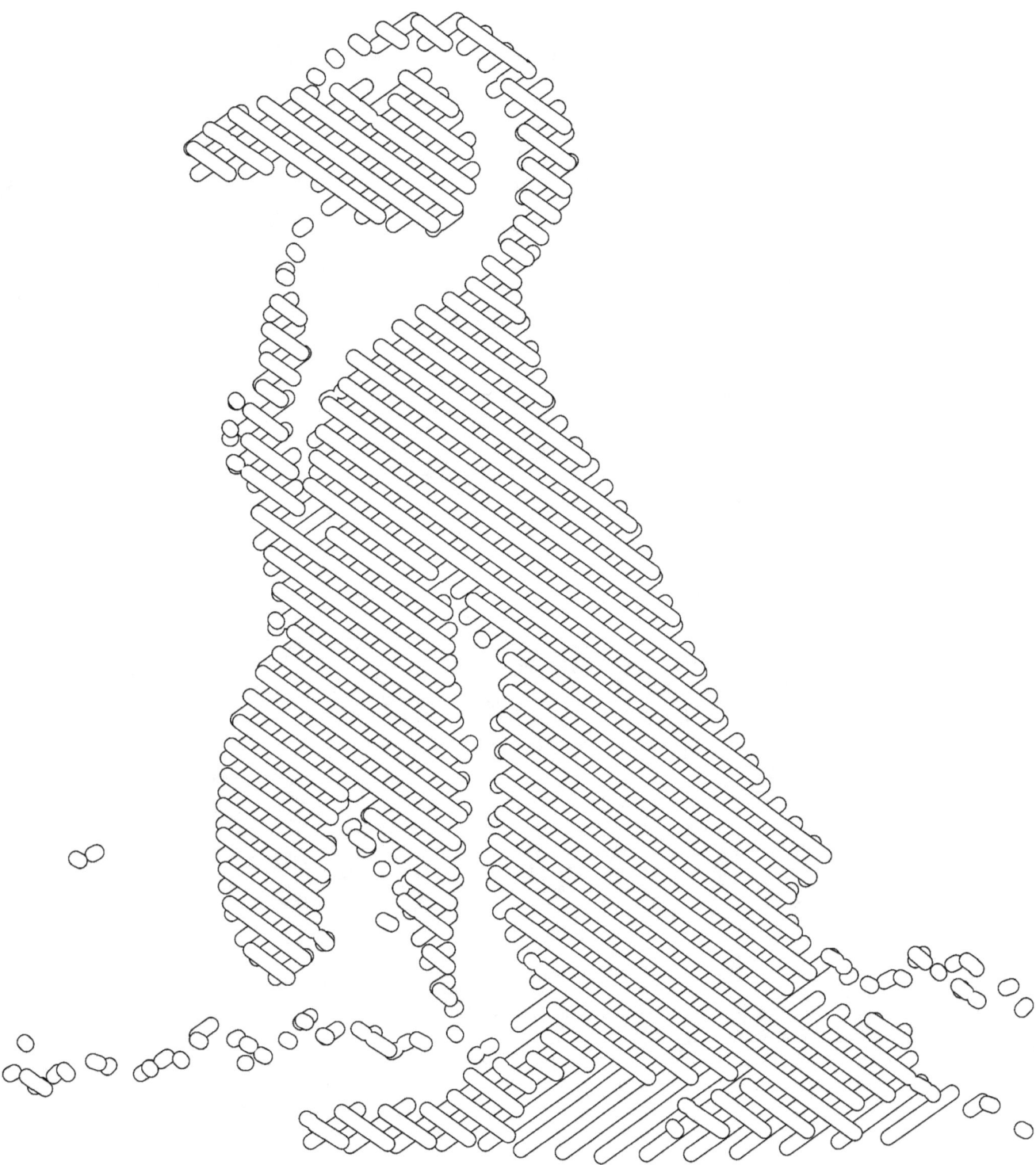

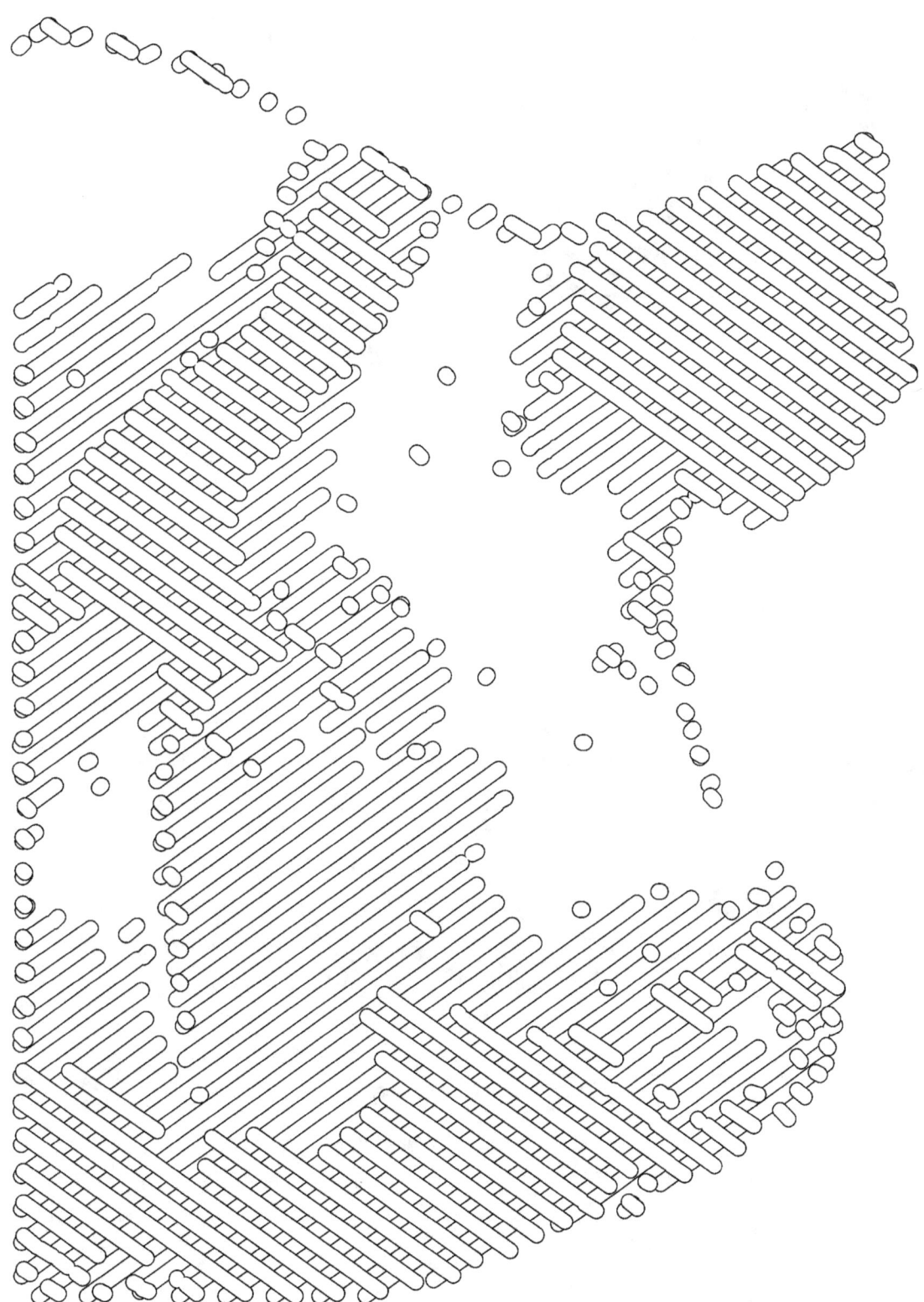

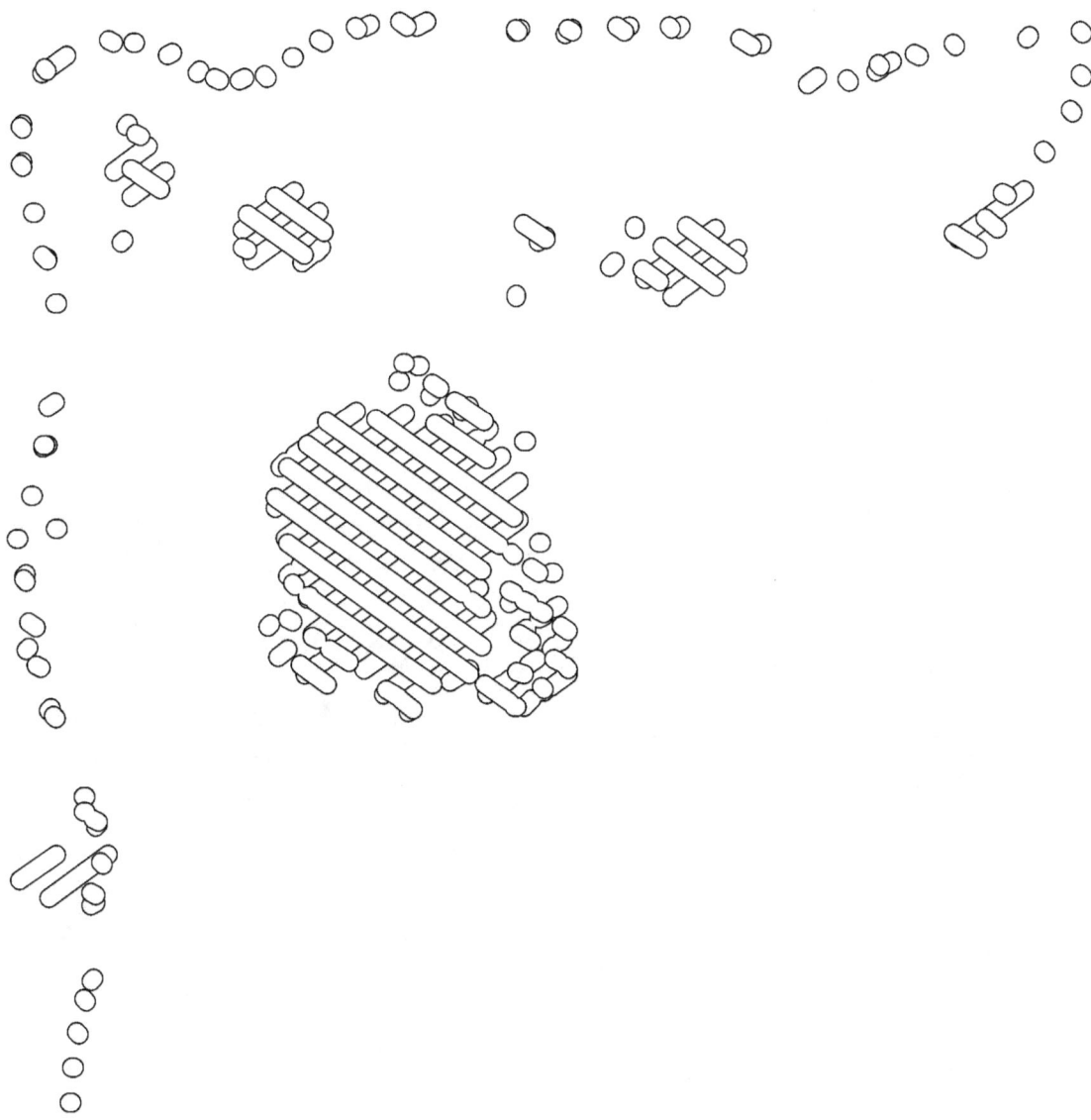

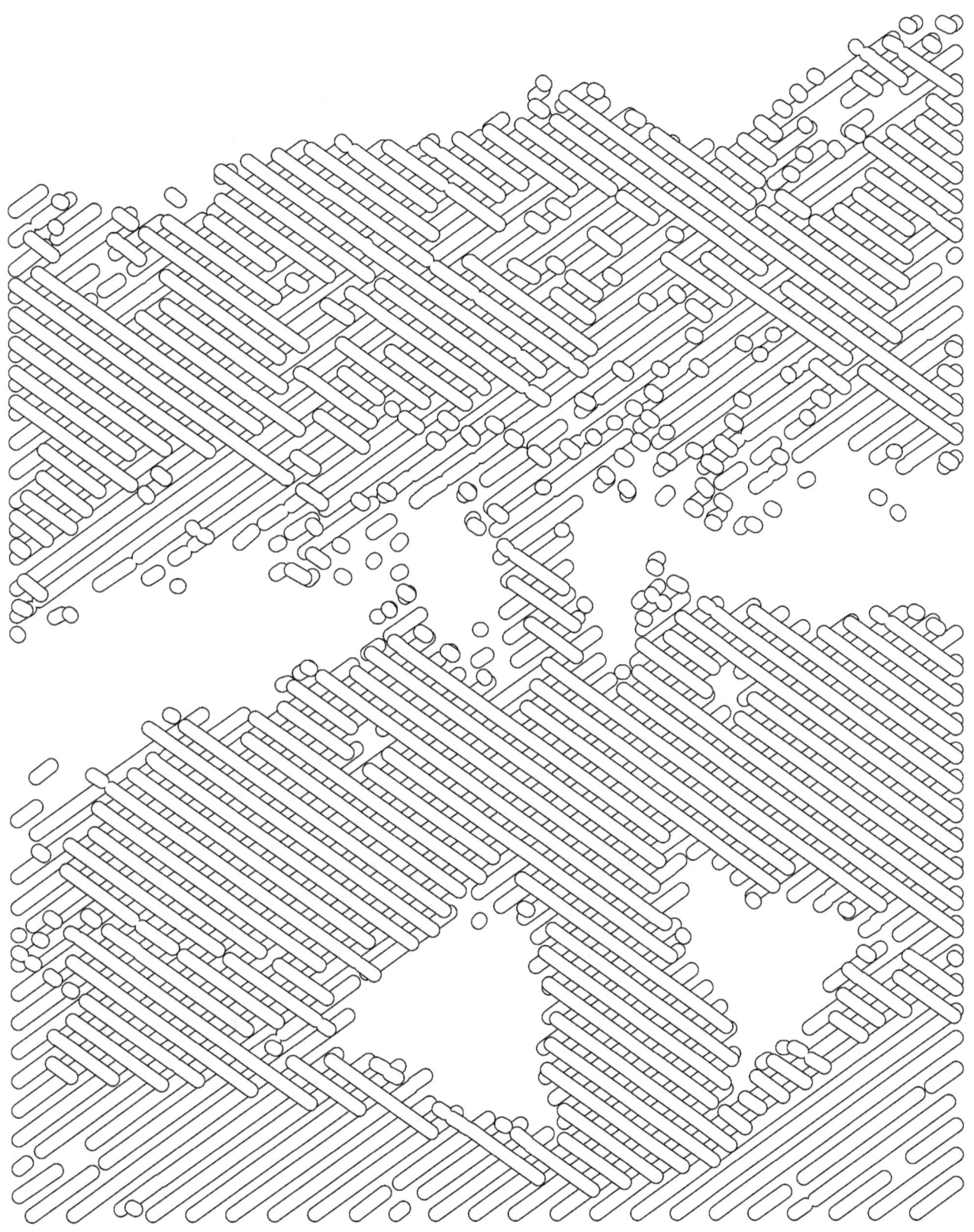

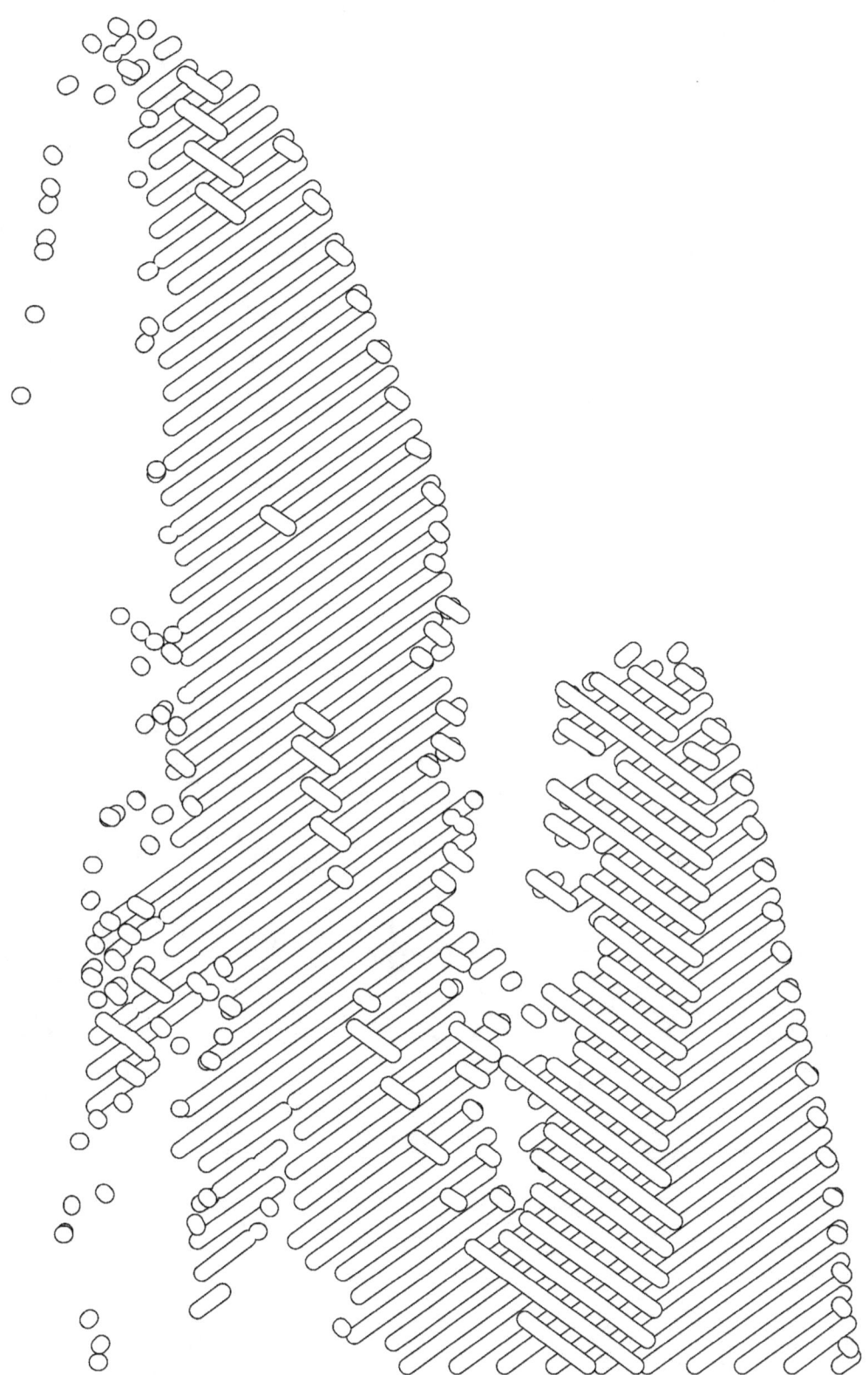

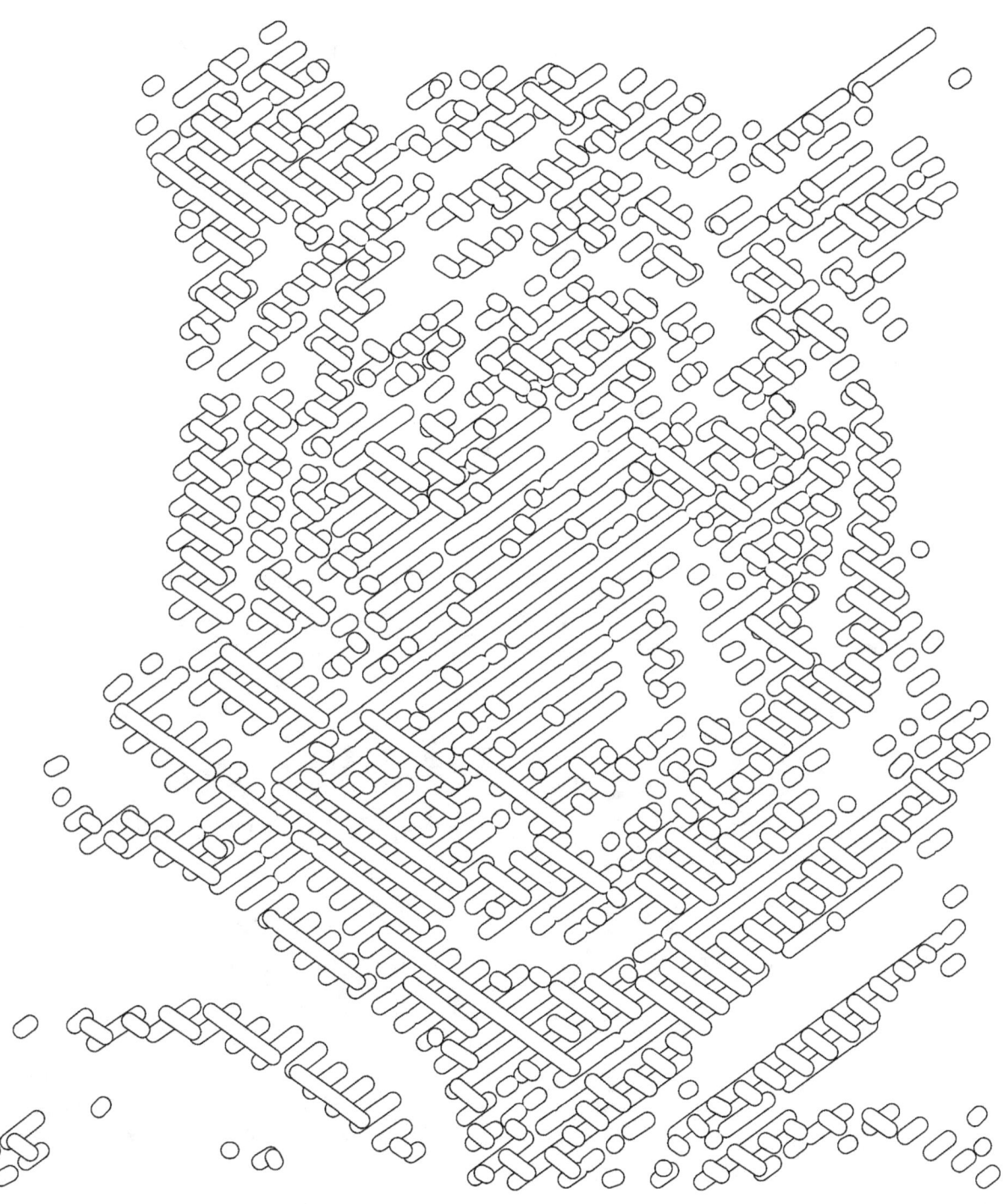

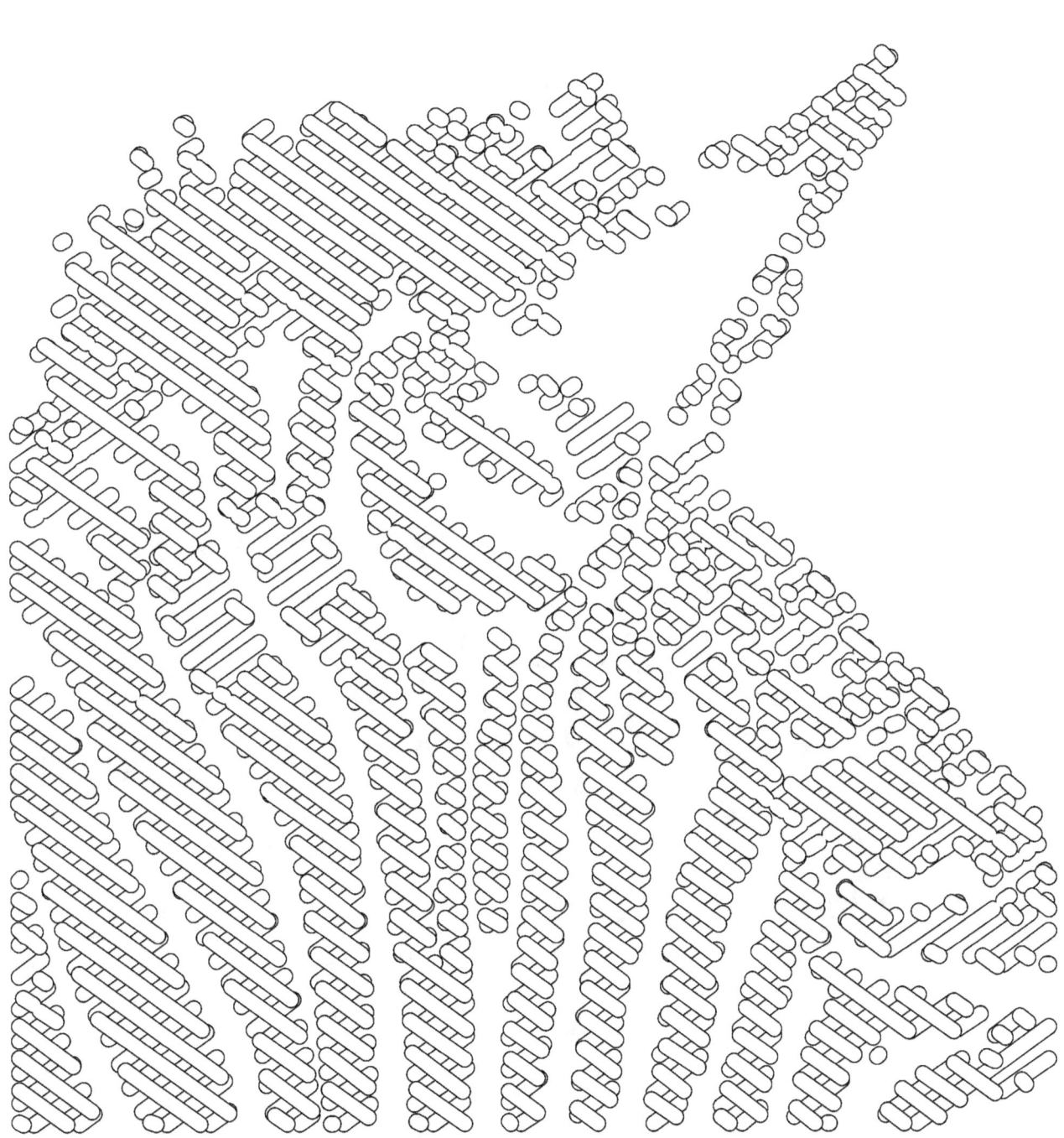